FORESIGHT

Unleashing the Power of
Your Psychic Gifts to Predict the Future

DAVID KNIGHT

FORESIGHT

First published by DPK Publishing—AscensionForYou 2022

A CIP catalogue record for this book is available from the British library.

The author of this book does not dispense or prescribe the use of any technique as a form of treatment for physical, emotional, or medical problems without the advice from a physician either directly or indirectly. The intent of the author is only to offer information of a general nature to aid your search for emotional and spiritual well-being. In the event you use any of the information in this book for yourself or others, the author does not assume responsibility for your actions.

ISBN: 978-1914936-19-7 (Paperback)
ISBN: 978-1914936-21-0 (eBook)
ISBN: 978-1914936-20-3 (Hardcover)

Cover artwork by: 100covers, 100covers.com
Editing by: Nina Shoroplova, ninashoroplova.ca
Typesetting by: Amit Dey, amitdey2528@gmail.com

www.AscensionForYou.com

OCC006000 **BODY, MIND & SPIRIT** / Dreams
OCC007000 **BODY, MIND & SPIRIT** / Parapsychology / ESP (Clairvoyance, Precognition, Telepathy)
OCC008000 **BODY, MIND & SPIRIT** / Divination / Fortune Telling

If you enjoy reading, **FORESIGHT** . . . download *Deliverance of Love, Light, and Truth* for free when you join David's mission for a 'full and blissful life'.

Visit: AscensionForYou.com

Dedication

To God, my 'spirit guides' and the ethereal beings who provide
me with knowledge and wisdom and protection and love
during my earth-plane sojourn ... and upon many different
planes and dimensions and realms of existence.

Epigraph

"Where God's Almighty Power meets man's
undoubting faith there is a holy marriage
of which miracles are born."

—Charlotte Sharman

"What matters is to live in the present, live now, for very moment is now.
It is your thoughts and acts of the moment that creates your future.
The outline of your future path already exists,
for you created its pattern by your past."

—Sia Baba

"Until you make the unconscious conscious,
it will direct your life and you will call it fate."

—Carl Jung

"God's goodness is flooding the universe all of the time,
but human consciousness is not receptive to it.
Therefore, blessings seem scarce."

—Thomas Hora

Contents

Introduction

Foreseeing the future

If you could foresee the future, would you consider that a gift or a curse? And would you then simply accept everything as 'whatever will be, will be', or try to live each day in the belief you can create the life you want for yourself and your loved ones around you?

Well, such questions may not be all you need to think about ... for there lies the problem, the confusion, and the uncertainty. You might bear witness to a future event, but the exact time and place and reason can remain unknown ... because the proof has not yet come to pass.

Besides such dilemmas, even when you know (deep inside your soul) that something will definitely happen, you'll still be wondering whether what is going to occur is simply fate or divine intervention. Why? Because of the many variables in between the time of your dream (or vision or forecast or prophecy) and when it takes place.

A whole host of things can influence the outcome, such as the choices that you—or other people—make. Then there is human error, karmic balance, free will, and cause and effect, to name a few. Even the statement 'no fate but what we make' provides a potential conflict of ideas, opinions, and possibilities. If an individual makes a decision that affects another's life, how can one deem that they have made their own choice? Surely karma has to be involved, doesn't it?

So, observing what's going to take place may neither empower you in any way, shape, or form nor provide you with the ability to prevent it from occurring, even if you want to, or feel that you should. Perhaps we're just not meant to determine the outcome, even if a moral compass were at our disposal.

Allow me to expand on this.

Over many years, I have become a channel for 'spirit', for which I have developed automatic writing (also called *channelling* or *inner dictation*). I believe this is a spiritual gift.

On one occasion, my consciousness was being taken to some crossroads. 'Do you turn left, or right, or onward? And how do you know whether any—or all—routes won't lead to the same destination? One may be quicker, another more joyous, and a third may be laced with trepidation and fear.'

The answer soon became clear ... simply keep moving. After all, it is believed that most things in life result from our own choices and free will, but are they made with faith and hope and trust, so they can create a destiny within truth, too?

And what makes you think and feel you are always the 'doer'? Can you really believe that this is the case ... especially if God is giving you the skill, chance, power, fortune, time, space, cause, health, and the body and soul and mind to achieve what you think you want and need?

Now let's delve deeper.

Throughout history, people have sought the wisdom of foresight, seeking guidance from soothsayers, fortune tellers, seers, psychics, and mediums, to name but a few. It seems the desire to discover hidden knowledge or foresee future events captivates our imaginations and poses countless further questions. Is life predetermined? Are our lives planned on a soul level and lived out on the physical plane? Is God a master puppeteer? How much control do we really have in our daily existence? Is everything preordained? Do we really have free will?

Consider that line I mentioned earlier: 'No fate but what we make', taken from the classic 1980s film, *The Terminator*. From a precognitive point of view, this is a real conundrum. I mean, on one hand, you could assume the future is a blank slate. On the other, those who experience such things witness (or feel) that something will take place. It is certain. It is fixed, and so it appears to be fate.

One could state that a prime example of 'fate' was the experience of Jesus Christ ... and that what he went through was both necessary and ordained by God. He acted out his destiny to guide people from the depths of shadow into the light. One could say he was the greatest prophet known to man because he knew for certain when, where, and how his earthly body would die. And his resurrection too!

We need to clarify that the one who prophesies 'speaks to people' to both encourage and motivate. We often use the noun *prophecy* to explain a feeling (or sensing) of what is going to happen—something based on what we believe—instead of taking existing facts into account. Know that *prophecy* is actually a Greek word meaning to declare divine will, to interpret, and to make known the truth of God, rather than meaning to predict the future.

We could expand this further.

For God's will to constantly unfold, then one's karma must surely play a role, because all life and energy require balance upon the scales of justice. Consider the 'perceived' good and bad in thought and word and deed, the positive and negative, love and hate, and truth versus lies; all these affect both the individual and the masses.

Spirit once asked me to imagine a row of bells in a variety of shapes and sizes. They chime and ring in different waves of pitch and tone, and each reverberates and echoes. Our life experiences resemble this, and our future will usually reflect our past deeds karmically too. From this, there is no escape. So, each of us is, in fact, the orchestrator of the bells and the music is our 'deeds'. The result of which allows every soul free will, with choices and decisions to make both day and night, which can be deemed spontaneous or fateful.

The *Titanic's* maiden voyage

Now let's consider human error, karma, divine intervention, natural laws, and fate in an example where perhaps all of these played their part: the sinking in the North Atlantic of RMS *Titanic* on her maiden voyage. A quick overview of the facts reminds us that the famous White Star liner struck an iceberg at 11.40 pm on 14 April 1912 and sank in the early hours of 15 April 1912. However, what occurred before it set sail and up to the period after the sinking—resulting in the loss of some 1500 lives—is a tragic event full of what ifs and why nots.

At the British inquest into the sinking of the *Titanic,* one of the first big talking points was the disregard by Sir John Charles Bigham, Lord Mersey (overseer of the inquest), for the evidence submitted by the survivors of the fire crew. Apparently, there had been a fierce blaze in one of the 300-tonne coal bunkers for possibly as long as two weeks prior to the ship leaving the port of Southampton. Imagine how many passengers would have declined the trip if they had known that! World-renowned specialists have since stated that the temperature would have reached 1000° Celsius … hot enough to buckle and weaken the first watertight compartment at its base. They believe this reduced the strength of the steel to 25 per cent! A fire crew had to battle this by emptying the bunker and disposing of the coal in the engine's boilers. Worse was to come, for during the Atlantic voyage another fire broke out in a second bunker. This was also extinguished, but the effects of both fires forced Captain Smith's hand and caused him to take an ill-fated gamble.

Another ship, the *Mesaba,* sent iceberg warnings to *Titanic's* wireless room at 9.52 pm *Titanic* time 'From Mesaba to Titanic. In latitude 42° N to 41° 25', longitude 49° W to longitude 50° 30' W, saw much heavy pack ice and great number large icebergs, also field ice, weather good, clear.'

This warning was not relayed to the bridge, though Captain Smith would have known about the risk of icebergs, anyway. He allowed the course to head further south.

However, he did have to weigh up the small chance of a collision with an iceberg with the fact that, because of the fires, there would not be enough coal to make sure the *Titanic* reached New York unless she maintained her speed. It would have been commercial suicide if the ship had completely run out of fuel … let alone not arrived on time.

This vital information has always been brushed under the carpet. Joseph Bruce Ismay, an English businessman who served as chairman and managing director of the White Star Line, survived the sinking and knew how relevant the fires were. Before the US inquest started, Ismay was desperately trying to get any surviving members of the fire crew back to the UK, preventing this information from getting out. He even tried to disguise telegram. requests (to and from the offices) with coded messages using his surname in reverse—Yamsi.

In addition, what if there had been binoculars in the crow's nest instead of being locked in a cupboard? But even without these, perhaps lookouts Fredrick Fleet and Reginald Lee could have spotted the iceberg sooner, had it not been such a calm sea.

What about the *Titanic* wireless operator who did not relay a message from SS *Californian* that she had earlier become surrounded by ice and had to stop temporarily. Apparently, the wireless operator was so inundated with passenger messages to the mainland that he even told his *Californian* counterpart to 'Shut up. Shut up. I am busy.' It's no surprise that the steamship operator responded in kind by turning off his equipment and going to bed, which is why he subsequently never received the CQD (a distress signal used in the early 1900s, Come Quick Disaster) sent out later by the *Titanic*.

Then there's the uncertainty of which ship was closest, the SS *Californian* or RMS *Carpathia* or even a mystery vessel whose lights were seen between the *Titanic* and the *Californian*. Much speculation surrounds this theory that those who perished could have received help much sooner. A Norwegian sailing ship called the *Samson* has frequently come up during investigations. If true, it would have probably been hunting seals, which was considered poaching and illegal, making it quite plausible that it ignored the distress rockets for fear of being caught.

There is still no proof this occurred though, despite checks into record logs. Hence, it was Captain Stanley Lord and his crew of the *Californian*, deemed to be only five miles (eight kilometres away), who were believed guilty of ignoring those rockets of distress. But here is another twist in the sad tale. New evidence has since emerged that that may not be true after all!

Perhaps the mystery ship was, in fact, SS *Mount Temple*! The plot thickens. We need to remember that the exact location of where the *Titanic* sank was not actually established until 1 September 1985, and it correlates to Captain Lord's testimony that the *Californian* was between seventeen and twenty miles (less than 30 kilometres) away, which then proved his navigational skills were spot on, and he was where he said he was.

In addition, Captain Moore of the *Mount Temple* was told by his company superiors not to venture into the ice field under any circumstances, basically ignoring *Titanic*'s plight. In what seems an attempt to disguise *Mount Temple*'s location, that steamship's logbook omits passenger and crew claims that they spotted the *Titanic*. Stranger still, notes and pages and entries made to the log went missing after the event.

What finally appears to vindicate Captain Lord's claim are two pieces of compelling evidence dated almost five years apart. Joseph Groves Boxhall, the fourth office of the *Titanic*, noted in the log that the mystery ship had 'two masts close together', which was most unusual. During the First World War, SMS *Möwe*, a German navy 'raider' commanded by Nikolaus zu Dohna-Schlodien, spotted, and sank the *Mount Temple* on 16 December 1916. This was recorded in a top secret German war diary, using the same phrase: 'two masts close together'. Subsequently, in April 1992, James Decoverly, Deputy Chief of Marine Accidents in the UK at the time, considered the *Californian*'s position was between seventeen and twenty miles (less than thirty kilometres) from the *Titanic* at the time of the collision and so was NOT the so-called mystery ship.

Now let's consider three further facts. Reportedly, the *Titanic* could stay afloat with up to four of its sixteen watertight compartments breached: the impact breached five. Incidentally, the breached compartments were precisely where the first bunker fire took place!

After the collision, the *Titanic* did not immediately stop. Why not? This is alarming news, especially when almost 500 tonnes of water a minute were being forced against the breach. This might have affected the calculation of its final 'position' too. (This is based on *Titanic*'s last known position, adjusted by time, speed, current, and direction and to transmit those co-ordinates).

Was Captain Smith's order to set a dead reckoning inaccurate?

In addition, why had no lifeboat drills been carried out? Was it the intense fear and panic that led to launching the lifeboats without full capacity? And many years later, examination of retrieved parts of the liner from the depths of the ocean (together with paperwork in the archives) led to the possibility that low-quality steel or weak rivets had been used, which may have contributed to the sinking too.

In addition to all these issues, witnesses and survivors stated that starlight disguised the calamity. You would think the exact opposite and believe a clear and calm night is to your advantage ... until we learn of a phenomenon known as 'scintillation'. These unique atmospheric conditions produce an uneven refraction of starlight whereby layers of warm and cold air cause lights to flicker with rapid changes of brightness in the twinkling of stars and—wait for it—even in radio sources. Is this another reason that the nearby ship didn't realise it was *Titanic*'s Morse signal lamps and never came to her aid? Was this trick of light the final nail in *Titanic*'s coffin?

Thank goodness, then, for Captain Arthur Rostron of the *Carpathia* who sped through an ice field from sixty miles (around 100 kilometres) away. He increased his speed from 14.5 knots per hour to 18 knots, saving an hour's journey to the stricken ship, arriving at 4 am to help rescue some 705 survivors. A point to note is that Rostron, a religious man, said, 'I can only conclude another hand than mine was on the helm.' Very poignant indeed.

So, when I look at these things in greater detail, it makes me wonder whether the ship of dreams ever stood a chance at all. I mean, one 'negative' thing after the other, a catalogue of human errors, and a bizarre set of circumstances. It's easy to see why this tragedy could be deemed as the hand of fate. Although the responsibility appears to lie at Captain Smith's door, one may wonder whether he was wholeheartedly to blame. And, for all the pain and suffering, could those natural laws of creation, or even God's will, have dictated the outcome? Was it destiny? Karma? If so, isn't this a miracle itself?

Spiritual destiny

Interestingly, I was asked during a meditation once to think about destiny from a spiritual point of view, to consider that the goal—through a person's self-realization of their own divinity—is to reach fulfilment, bliss, and peace in God. This premise should therefore circumnavigate every sinew of our being.

I was also informed that during our earthly sojourns—our soul journeys—we need to remember and appreciate the 'time' we are given, which has to be used for love and growth not only for ourselves but within society too. We need to understand that all societies live or fall by their connection to the core values of peace, good conduct, and righteousness. Therefore, it is our own choice and so-called free will that dissipates, dilutes, and filters good actions from bad ... the effect from the cause.

So, as you make your way through life, can you choose to trust in yourself and simply let go ... or, moreover, let God? Or will you continue to seek to control every outcome and aspect of your life? If it's the latter, then you may become tempted to explore other ways to bear witness to the truth and turn to the many forms of divination available to you.

You could start predicting the future using some well-known examples, including reading tea leaves, Tarot cards, rune stones, or auras. How about using psychometry, palm-reading, or scrying, or throwing three coins to consult the I Ching? An important thing to note here is that when you are invoking energies within and around you, one must first cleanse your thoughts—and the objects used—through prayer, invocations, or affirmations.

Alternatively, to receive the guidance you need, you could simply turn 'within'. You do not need to spend any money ... or travel anywhere. You could even pick a flower, gaze upon its beautiful petals, and delve deep into your heart—and creation—to seek the answers you need.

Know that meditation provides you with the opportunity to go beyond the boundaries of your senses too. Please appreciate this: any form of inner inquiry will always bring you closer to your goal and create a real link to your subconscious mind (and soul), whereby you expand your connection with God.

Heck, you could simply trust your intuition and those gut feelings that will also lead you towards your higher good. An old saying states the 'tummy' knows best! Of course, it is fine for me to state this, but most people believe the future can't be seen or known. And many academics and scholars will also insist dreams and visions are caused by psychiatric or neurological conditions. They regard everything about the future as speculation upon present information. In fact, mainstream science does not support such practices as reliable methods for predicting the future, basically because the 'results' are not physically 'observable'. And therein lies the main problem—a lack of evidence.

So, where and how do you find irrefutable proof? Well, our modern and technological age gives us all an advantage. We have the internet, newspapers, and radio. Cameras and mobile phones can now capture photographs, dates, and times of events, which can collaborate information or 'predictions' that previous generations never could. A privileged position indeed!

That said, this made little difference for two prominent people with special 'gifts' ... Joan of Arc and Nostradamus. So, let's take a brief look into why they inspire our hearts, captivate our imaginations, and still enthral many lives today.

Joan of Arc

Jeanne d'Arc (Joan of Arc) was a famous visionary who was also known as "The Maid of Orléans." She testified that her first vision took place while she was in her father's garden in 1425, when she was about thirteen (history has recorded the date of her birth as 6 January 1412). The vision, involving Saint Michael surrounded by angels, brought her to tears. For my part, this confirms true insight—the emotional aspect proves it was genuine. It is important to understand that dreams and imagery involving God—and God's Hierarchy of Light—are real rather than imagined.

Joan continued to receive many more visions of saints and immense heavenly guidance through her heart and soul. It's no wonder then that two of her prophecies circulated around the country during challenging times of war. One promised that a maid from the borderlands of Lorraine would come forth to work miracles. The other was that France had been lost by a woman … but would be restored by a virgin. In 1429, she influenced events so much that her presence and visions turned the Anglo-French conflict into a religious war, creating devotion and the hope of divine help. Joan had the faith of the troops: they fervently believed she could bring them to victory, and she did!

However, she was eventually captured by some French nobles who were allies of the English. During May 1430, she was handed over, imprisoned in the keep of a castle, and tried for heresy, which was clearly politically motivated. Nevertheless, even when threatened with torture and facing death by fire, she still insisted that voices of God guided her. This is faith in action. Almost a year later, when she was aged about 19, on the 30 May 1431, Joan was burned at the stake.

After her death, she became known as a heroine of the Hundred Years' War. In 1456, Pope Callixtus III debunked the charges against her. After pronouncing her innocent, he proclaimed her a martyr. In 1803, Napoleon declared her a national symbol of France. She was 'blessed' by the Catholic church in 1909 and canonized in 1920, and Joan of Arc became one of nine patron saints of France.

For me, she's the perfect example of someone living without fear, with the knowledge that God's love will guide her to whatever end. It's well-known that she was illiterate and could not use the 'written' word to defend herself. In reality, the words from her heart were from the eternal witness of truth. Truly, Joan was beyond ego and lived without attachment to the 'body'.

Nostradamus

Moving on now to Michel de Nostredame, a man better known as Nostradamus. Born to a grain dealer in 1503 in Lyon, Southern France, he was a visionary. He had Jewish heritage, but his father converted to Christianity. Interestingly, it's said that his grandfather was also a 'seer', so it seems likely that not only do we all inherit our DNA, characteristics, and elements of our health and well-being through our lineage, we may also inherent our latent powers (spiritual and psychic gifts).

Nostradamus married in 1531. His wife and two children later died of the bubonic plague in 1534, which was said to be the catalyst for his abilities of foresight. This resonates deeply within me because time and time again, we hear about people who develop their spiritual gifts or experience psychic phenomena after emotional, physical, or mental trauma. Many people who have also gone through near-death experiences have documented their visions or wonderful meetings with saints, guardian angels, and Jesus; they feel blessed by moments of immense peace and love within 'heaven'.

After his wife and children died, Nostradamus travelled through France and then Italy. When he returned to France in 1545, he assisted Louis Serre, a prominent physician in the fight against a major Black Death outbreak in Marseille … and then outbreaks of the disease in Salon-de-Provence on his own. In 1547, he settled there and married a rich widow and had six children—three sons and three daughters. He later revisited Italy, whereby he moved away from medicine toward the occult.

In the 1550s, he published an almanac to great success, and then began his work as an astrologer for wealthy patrons and even royalty. It's weird how he became so successful, because he was also heavily criticized by professional astrologers who thought he was incompetent!

Nostradamus made his predictions and forecasting events using 'judicial' astrology, (God's judgment through the stars), calculating planetary and stellar bodies and their relationship to the Earth. This form of astrology was very prominent at that time but was considered a heresy by the Catholic Church. The prophecies were based on consistent night and day observations of the 'heavens'—the changing positions of the sun and moon, the fluctuations in the brightness of the planets and their paths within constellations, and the path of asteroids, comets, and so on.

This wasn't new, of course, as such observation is an ancient tradition. Throughout history, we have used such information gathered from the stars to plan 'life' by day and night; for instance, sowing and harvesting crops, and also for avoiding impending disasters! Even today, we still have daily horoscopes in newspapers, though how serious one takes these are down to the individual.

Nostradamus then began writing his predictions in one thousand quatrains, four-line stanzas, producing 942 of these before his death. It took about four years to complete and collate them into a book entitled *Les Prophéties*, known in English as *The Prophecies of Nostradamus*. Between 1555 and 1568, his quatrains were a series of four-line poems published in groups of a hundred and called 'centuries'. Nostradamus's problem was that he feared persecution from religious establishments, so he wrote these verses in a way to obscure their meaning ... yet still leave clues for future generations. There were also uplifting predictions to the Queen, though that might have been a way of protecting himself! The Queen of France, Catherine de' Medici, was the first to read his work in 1555.

Because of the turbulent and perilous times of civil war, risk of invasion, death, and disease, much of his work has an antichrist theme and hints at deeds yet to be carried out by Napoleon and Hitler, calling him Hister, the German child of the Rhine.

Nostradamus believed in the cycle of time itself and the repetitions of tragedies, disasters, and wars. He hoped the world would learn from its mistakes, and surely wanted the reader to look inwards and take life and their future in their own hands.

This poetry of prediction had an almost rhythmic effect on the mind as he used anagrams, poetic disguises, wordplay, and phrases that appear random and yet are ordered. In addition, hidden codes and arcane symbols appear to speak to the human brain, while others seem completely nonsensical. I guess that's why about 30 per cent of his quatrains have still to be linked with any 'evidence'. Some are so obscure they could have been referring to his present or our future. Only time will tell if his predictions are of potential catastrophes ... but a 70 per cent so-called 'hit' rate is amazing! Therefore, in times of unrest, or even when the naturally gullible see the forecasts have been contradicted, the power of prophecy can endure for centuries.

There seems no let-up in the fascination with Nostradamus, especially the way the world is currently progressing. Because of the ever-increasing droughts, floods, and famine across the globe, a greater number of people are seeking to use 'prophecy' to prepare and safeguard our future well-being. In addition, his prophecies might be used to help ease the religious tensions between different faiths and nations, to alleviate hatred, terrorism, and war.

On the other side of the coin, sceptics will still argue that you could make anything match the sixteenth century verses. The issue here is that we could see them as simple suggestions of such events, and that the nature of history appears to make his predictions come true. One may therefore relate to dates and information from the past and merely attempt to decode and attribute them to the future. People have also stated the only prediction he ever got right was on the evening of 1 July 1566 when he allegedly told his secretary Jean Aimé de Chavigny, 'You will not find me alive at sunrise.' The next morning, he was reportedly found dead between his writing desk and his bed. The cause was dropsy (an abnormal swelling of tissues from a build-up of fluid). They aged him 63.

So, do you think his predictions for the future are fixed, awaiting the right moment to arrive? Or were his visions simply warnings for humanity to change course? For example, Quatrain 1, 69 appears to signify an asteroid strike. Is he sending us a warning? Can people be proactive? In another, he 'predicts' the end of the world will take place in 3797, Armageddon. Well, you and I won't be around for that one!

A Global Database

When you think about it, the only real choice we ever have to make is our own. Therefore, the question here is whether you believe everything is set in stone. Or are we our own creators, whereby we can finally learn from our past to create the future we want for ourselves?

For any doom and gloom mongers amongst us, one further possibility to help preserve and protect the planet for generations to come is a computer-based Nostradamus! There is technology called GDELT, which stands for Global Database of Events, Language, and Tone. Kalev Leetaru (of Yahoo and Georgetown University) created this project that revolves around a 'super' computer, which is continually being updated with information from around the world.

Apparently, GDELT currently contains a data set of more than 11.3 billion metadata entity annotations from 280 million records on news articles, human societal-scale (interpersonal contact) behaviour and beliefs, organizations, and nations. It's a multilingual search and analytical project that looks for patterns, trends, relationships, emotions, and forecasts events too. I find this more disconcerting than any of Nostradamus's predictions.

I gather it gets updated every minute, bridging geography and language to watch the world in real time. Whilst I am sure there are many reasons for the good that GDELT may do to help the human race, it is still based on grammatical, statistical, and machine-based algorithms.

Everything has its place, I know, but 'technology' and I don't get on. I'm not sure how many times over the years I have wanted to get a hammer and smash my laptop to bits or throw it out of the window! So, will the world ever be ready to completely trust in AI? Would you ever want (or allow) Big Brother to dictate your own future? I think it's better to rely wholeheartedly on God.

This brings me to myself and my own experiences. Nearly thirty years have passed since Spirit first called on me, and some people might be curious as to why I have waited all this time to tell my story. Well, throughout my continued spiritual guidance and education, I've learned that timing is everything. Perhaps, subconsciously, I was also concerned what people might think of me. But times have changed a lot since the early 1990s, and not much seems to shock the world these days.

Of course, it will be down to others to accept or deny what I convey. After all, anyone can make things up, manipulate images, and share 'fake' news, can't they? However, we need to realise the truth is not so much in the eye of the beholder but inside the heart of the beholder.

I recall the first time I received a clairaudient communication from Spirit in 1993. It occurred when my father popped in for a cup of tea. (He always tried to stop by on a Saturday morning). We spoke about my grandma as she was poorly. Dad explained he thought she didn't have long before she'd pass. As I opened the fridge to get the milk, a voice spoke to me (as if in my head and not in my ear), 'She will cross over on Wednesday.' This took me by total surprise. It hadn't happened before, and I felt dumbstruck, because I didn't know what to say or do with the information. Grandma passed exactly when the voice said she would. But I never told my father this, and I am not sure why.

Now here's an interesting update to the above information. I am actually writing this on Tuesday 21 December 2021 and I wanted to provide the exact dates, but I just could not remember them! So, yesterday I spent nearly three hours searching online with different birth, death, and marriage records, including in Ancestry, Findmypast, and MyHeritage websites. But I could not get a one hundred per cent match for Grandma's passing. Very frustrating indeed.

Researching her death made me think about those times when I was a kid visiting my grandparents at the east coast town of Brightlingsea in the UK. Whether this reminiscing had a role to play I don't know, but at about 4 a.m. this morning I had a dream in which I was by the shore of a crystal clear sea. There were some buildings ahead, and I soon found myself inside what felt like a hotel or a seaside guest house. I went up some stairs and then went through a door to a corridor. I had a key in my hand and stood between two white wooden doors, number ten on one side to my right and number eleven on the other side behind me. I looked at number eleven, then the ten again … and it felt as though I was waiting for something. Perhaps I had to decide which room to enter, but just as I was about to use the key for number ten, I woke up!

I thought about the dream for a while and kept thinking about the numbers. There is a saying that 'Spirit does not waste', so I knew they had to be relevant. As I was on holiday for Christmas break, I went up to the attic to search through my father's files. I had a recollection that there were some documents about Grandma inside them. And lo and behold, a few minutes later, I found her funeral service remembrance sheet! On the front was the date she passed away, 10 November 1993 … so the ten in the dream referred to the day, and the eleven was the month. But perhaps the numbers on the doors also signified the eleventh day of the month when she was born and the tenth when she exited her mortal coil. Wow!

So, looking back, my dad came by our house for his cup of tea on the Saturday (which would have been 6 November 1993), and Grandma died on the exact day spirit had told me she would: Wednesday, 10 November 1993!

Something else to note here was that in the remembrance service booklet there is a poem entitled, 'My Mother Believed in Me'. I think Dad selected it. The last verse is below, and it mentions the 'crystal sea', as in my dream from early this morning!

My dear old mother has gone from me,
To dwell by the crystal sea,
If I ever go to her side, 'twill be,
Because my mother believed in me!

I had not seen this poem since I was nineteen years old, and I feel so blessed that my grandma, my dad, or a 'spirit guide' helped me with this information. It's more proof that God truly is our eternal witness and how important it is to differentiate between having an insightful dream and having one that shows you have received information from spirit, from God, and should therefore enact upon it! Obviously, the dream last night was meant to be. Time and time again, life will give us what we need ... which is not necessarily what we think we want.

One might describe both types of dreams, and psychic abilities, as if they are some precursors to greatness, but I believe that we all possess such gifts. One must remember, though, that the ego plays no part in our soul's goal of self-realization—it's all just a matter of tuning into the right frequencies, of resonating with the particular energy. No wonder we have the term *medium wave*!

(Here is an old picture of my dad and Grandma).

"MY MOTHER BELIEVED IN ME!"

"When I was a little mischievous lad,
The neighbors would all agree
That I must be going straight to the bad,
But mother believed in me!

And just because she believed in me,
I could't be mean, you see;
For it helps a boy to do right when he
Can say, 'My mother believes in me.'

"To me, as a man, how often there came
Temptations from which I'd flee!
The reason, you know, was always the
    same—
That mother believed in me.

And so, because she believed in me,
I wouldn't do wrong, you see;
For to disappoint her – ah, that would
    be
To bad, when mother believed in me!

"It is not the least of blessings I've had
While passing thro' life, that she,
Though once I was such a mischievous
    lad,
Could always, believe in me.

My dear old mother has gone from me
To dwell by the Crystal Sea;
If I ever go to her side, 'twill be
Because my mother believed in me!"

                                    —Selected

Journaling my dreams

I'll now trace my steps back a little further to 1992.

After I became involved in meditation and healing development circles, I dreamt four or five times most nights. I would often lie awake, contemplating them, mulling them over, trying to decipher the images and feelings they brought into my heart and mind. I soon learned that when I am viewing events in a dream or meditation it seems to be either informative or precognitive; whereas, when I am actually within the scene itself, it appears I am being taught something.

The other thing is that people often say they have a 'key'—a symbol, a word, or an image—to help them identify precognition before, during, or after foreseeing an event. I believe my key is a flash of light at the start.

And I often see a newspaper within the dream, but more on this in a moment.

I could usually remember most—if not all—of a dream's details, but I soon wanted to keep a dream journal to record them, in case there were any patterns or pieces of information that needed further analysis. Eventually, late in 1995, I bought a pen with an inbuilt light around the nib ... 007 eat your heart out! Ha-ha. I kept it under my pillow with a notepad, so whenever I awoke from a dream, I could write and draw under the covers ... an essential system so as not to wake up my wife!

Over the years, I must have recorded thousands of dreams. It's interesting because the more I focused on them, the more I received. It's quite strange that when you place importance upon something—such as a spiritual gift—you will find it flourishes.

I also began having a few OBEs (out-of-body experiences), travelling on several occasions via astral projection to different planes of energy. I even received visitations from NBEs (non-biological entities) from other dimensions. In addition, I witnessed incredible UFOs ... but never captured any proof, which annoyed me greatly. When I think about what I'd seen, I wish smartphones were available back then. Having the ability to instantly capture evidence with a photograph or video clip would have been amazing ... a real game changer!

To experience such things is very humbling, and I am very grateful for everything that has flowed to me, through me, and from me.

And so, as bizarre as all this may seem, I urge that whatever you do in life, it should be done with passion and integrity and purpose and belief and truth, and especially with gratitude. Hold nothing back. Most successful artists or creatives, and those who reach the pinnacle in business, sports, finance (or in fact in any subject or task), usually state they needed to be fully committed and passionate, citing that without such an effort they would probably not have succeeded.

In contrast with these viewpoints though, perhaps you could also consider that true success is not always about the end result. A person who overcomes their challenges and simply gets through their day, someone who provides food for their family or has a roof over their head and a bed to sleep in at night, could deem that to be a great victory. Do you think or feel this way, too?

After a while, something very weird started to occur during my dreams and meditations.

The first occasion was during December 1992. I will call them flashes or flickers of light. Some were gentle and soft, while others had great intensity, like two or three bursts of a fluorescent blue-and-white lightning bolt. I felt them as they ripped through my consciousness … as if ripping through the fabric of time and space. Whether I was drifting during a sleep state or travelling across the ether at the time, I could always remember afterward this rather uncomfortable (but not painful) sensation taking place.

On very rare occasions, I would experience flashes of dark light, too. A friend who is a medium explained that those might have indicated that Spirit didn't want me to go anywhere at that precise time. Basically, Spirit was closing me down for my own protection.

In addition, five other types of light sometimes pierced through my head. On Tuesday, 18 January 1994, I experienced a conical flash; it resembled a pinprick of light that then zoomed outwards to create a larger circle. Next, it appeared rectangular in shape, then slightly on an angle … like a window moving from one dimension to another. The third type formed a doorway, with a slim light around the frame and a burst of light at the bottom. (An example of this came on Saturday, 22 January 1994.) The fourth type started as a soft glow of colour that burst with orange on the horizon. Finally, I experienced what I called a room flash—my whole mind briefly filled with brilliant white light.

In time, I learned the two-and three-step lightning bursts indicated precognition was taking place. Their unique intensity and sensation helped to differentiate them from my normal dreams.

On other occasions, I became aware of different precognitive 'keys', too. Common themes were reading a newspaper (or viewing one in the distance), looking through a window, and watching television.

These strange phenomena felt so profound that I wanted to try to find more information about them. I decided to delve deeper into the term *precognition* because it seemed to represent what I was going through. *Precognition* represents prescience, a vision of the future, or future sight, because the messages occur directly to the mind. The term derives from Latin: *pre* meaning 'prior to' and *cognition* meaning 'to gain knowledge'.

So, through precognition, one gathers information about an event that is yet to happen, through a feeling or a vision, or both. I guess you could also say it's clairvoyance, because it relates to an event or state not yet experienced. This often occurs to people while they are in a trance, a dream state, and during meditation. The results may also be described as fortune-telling, having second sight or foresight, or prophesying.

Allegedly, Aristotle used to study his prophetic dreams and proposed that they indicated that the dreamers' sense impressions were reaching forward to the event itself. Meanwhile, Democritus, a scientist and philosopher, suggested that emanations from future events could be sent back to the dreamer—an interesting viewpoint indeed. Well, his ideas certainly resonate with me!

Over the next few years, I realised the time between the flashes and dreams and the precognition event itself could be short or long. That said, my dream journal dating back to the early 1990s indicates the time could be anything from one day up to a month or more. This is fascinating ...

if we consider Nostradamus's quatrains seem to predict hundreds (and thousands) of years into the future!

So, you would think that it would have been easy for me to just sit back and wait for the proof. However, with long working hours and continually having to carry out home improvements, plus spending time with my wife and family and friends, I must have missed dozens of opportunities to compile more evidence. Back then, I had to rely on television news, articles on Ceefax late at night (remember that? ha-ha), and newspapers whenever I could get them.

Occasionally, I even overlooked confirmations that would have been financially beneficial to me. Spirit must have been trying to help us, because several times over the years, I had been given the name of a racing horse in a dream. But even though I would be looking every day in the sports section of a newspaper—to see if it was running—on the day it would run (and win), I would forget to buy the paper! Talk about looking a gift horse in the mouth, gee whiz!

As I mentioned earlier, please understand that God and Spirit never waste. So, there are always lessons to be learned. I am also aware of different levels of spiritual education and how some might view horse race winners as simply working at a lower or base level. But as I have said before, everything seems to happen for a reason.

Don't question this … please just trust it.

By the end of 1995, the frequency of my precognition activity increased substantially. What used to happen every six or eight weeks, happened every other week or so! Many images came through, perhaps to simplify the information I received. I became more confident at interpreting them; or rather, the spiritual details that were being relayed had greater detail, which allowed for a higher degree of accuracy. I always thought the scenes, images, and details must be correct, and it was only my perception that could possibly lead me astray!

Throughout these occurrences, I wondered, 'Where will all this lead?' Was the increase in activity for my benefit … and evidence of God's will and power and the natural laws of creation? Or were my precognitive dreams to provide additional proof for others? What other reasons could there be? I hoped one day there would be a definitive answer … and perhaps this book is it!

As you read through my dream log, answer these questions spontaneously for yourself. Would you like to explore your own psychic gifts and discover and access your intuition? What is happening in your life that provides you with evidence of God's creativity? Can you share that evidence with others? Will you share it with me? You can reach me at my website at AscensionForYou.com or connect through my social media channels.

P.S. To help you cross reference the dream log details with my original dream notes, the correlating sentences, which indicate precognition details, have been highlighted in yellow. These remain unedited to maintain their authenticity.

Stabbing

Method: Dream—Friday, 3 June 1994

Time before confirmation/evidence/proof: 7 days—Newspaper article Friday, 10 June 1994

Location/landmarks: Outside a building/pub? Wide curved road and path. Near a Town.

People: Group of men and women. A man with a knife. Main character— young woman.

Day or Night: Uncertain, I was observing, daytime, I think?

Scene: A woman violently stabbed, blood everywhere. Injuries from knife attack.

Colours: Light green (victim's dress)

Smells: N/A

Vehicles: White van? Ambulance?

Feelings: Panic/fear. The anguish of a woman.

Dream Log: I am viewing a building ... perhaps a hotel or bar/pub? A girl was wearing a low cut top (or dress)? ... though I thought she had been topless at some point? A man who appeared to have a ginger beard came into my mind. I was then suddenly looking at woman from behind, she had a lovely dress on, figure hugging, light green colour with gold specs all over it … like maybe an evening dress of some sort? The next second, she was lying on the floor covered in blood. I felt her anguish. She'd been stabbed in the stomach and was choking to death. Blood ran down her arms too. I could hear breathing as she struggled to pull herself off the ground … by pulling onto a vans bumper? What happened next seemed unbelievable. She appeared to stand up and go onto the path and walk away. (I took this to mean that she would live). I then woke up.

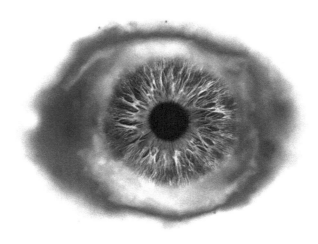

FRIDAY 3/6/94 Cont.

The first dream was very violent but some of it seems to have, could have been 'suggested' to what I had read in the newspaper earlier tonight.

In the local paper there was a public house that twice a week had 2 x topless Barmaids, apparently it was now packed on those days – The White Lion (somewhere) The two girls came from Derby.

Anyway in my dream a ~~a the girls~~ a girl who was in a low cut topless? dress or had been topless was somehow followed by a man – I just knew it was a man – I think with a ginger beard (came into my mind). I was suddenly looking at ~~this~~ a woman from behind, she had a lovely dress, figure hugging, light green colour with gold specs all over it, like maybe an evening dress of some sort? The next second she was lying on the floor covered in blood, I felt, it seemed to feel like I felt the anguish of her. She'd been stabbed in the stomach and was choking to death. Blood ran down her arms and I could hear ~~her~~ breathing as she struggled to pull herself off the ground by grabbing onto a VAN'S bumper.

The scene

BUTCHERS
PEOPLE
PATH
ROAD

TOWN?
AREA?

SOME SORT
VAN
(WHITE)

Now, what happened next seems unbelievable.
She then seemed to stand up, go to the path and walk away
(will he)

Seemed to get? up + walk away

A woman RIPPED open Blood everywhere

(Cont

FIEND KNIFES 5 WHO LAUGHED AT HIS GIRL'S PINK SHIRT

VIOLENT BRITAIN

By MARTYN SHARPE

Horror at pub

A MANIAC was on the run last night after he stabbed five students for laughing at his girlfriend's vivid pink T-shirt.

The knifeman lashed out in a pub garden as the mickey-taking youths celebrated the end of their exams.

His three victims collapsed with blood pouring from appalling injuries. Police were shocked by the latest act of violence to hit Britain.

Mark Thomas, 21, almost died from a collapsed lung.

A 20-year-old girl was knifed in the face, stomach and legs while a 20-year-old boy was slashed across the face.

The madman fled with his girlfriend — wearing a luminous pink top — running behind pushing her baby in a buggy.

Berserk

Four other students gave chase and wrestled the man to the ground outside a car showroom.

But he went berserk again, lashing out with a short-bladed knife.

Andrew Simpson, 25, was slashed in the face and stomach and another man needed 23 stitches in a face wound.

The maniac and his girlfriend, both in their 20s, then escaped.

Mark Thomas and Andrew Simpson were stable in hospital last night.

The other victims, who were not named, were said to be out of danger.

The drama started at the Pomona pub in Eccleshall Road, Sheffield.

A barmaid said: "The students were taking the mickey out of the woman's pink T-shirt and the man just snapped."

Police, who believe the knifeman is local, said: "Any one of the students could have died."

Conclusion: By gazing over my original copy of my 3 June 1994 scribble/drawing (writing is awful, I know) and from the newspaper report; the students were out celebrating … so perhaps the young woman's party dress is a clue? Unfortunately, I had no reference to the pink top of the 'attackers' girlfriend, though. The young woman stabbed in the stomach survived. What is interesting is that I found a photograph online today (22 December 2021) of the Pomona pub (which I think was later changed to Eccleshall Pub), though it might not even be there now. It has an almost identical look to my drawing, in particular a curved path and road in the foreground. Whether it looked the same way, back in '94, I'm not sure. Regarding predictive validity, I'd say this has a moderate correlation. But, if I was an investigative reporter, perhaps I could dig up some more information from those attacked, which would increase this. Unfortunately, a half-hour search online brought no further details other than this photo below.

PUB UTOPIA.com

PRECOGNITION 2

USAF Air Crash

Method: Meditation—Friday, 10 June 1994

Time before confirmation/evidence/proof: 16 days—Newspaper article 26 JUNE 1994

Location/landmarks: A tall monument and an open area but with structures nearby. USA?

People: N/A

Day or Night: Day

Scene: Clear blue sky. Plane flying/circling then turning on its side and crashing. Large explosion.

Colours: Grey. Black insignia or letters?

Smells: N/A

Vehicles: Very large aircraft.

Feelings: Feeling peaceful … and then shock!

Dream Log: I had allocated about an hour for my Friday meditation. I was so tired; I think I was drifting in and out of sleep state. But during it I received a couple of short 'vibrations' … energy/sound through my right eardrum … I knew spirit had started to communicate with me. Then sensing something drawing close ... a light? Not seeing it but feeling it. I decided to let my mind just drift.

I'd been in a rowing boat, passed through a tunnel and came to some steps. I climbed out of the boat, up the steps and then started to gaze out of a window. It appeared I was viewing some sort of large open area ... but linked to a town centre or city. There was a large monument in the centre of my 'view', and people were all walking about. There was a lady pushing a push chair/baby down the front. It was a nice day, and the sun was shining.

Suddenly, I had a weird feeling (and a thought and picture in my head) whilst looking out of the window. It was a large plane which was about to crash, it came (or would come) down on its wing after circling in the air. My vision came upon a hole (?) in the metal somewhere on the body or wing tail of the plane? It would crash and the figure of '263' came into my head. The event just disappeared (out of my head), and I was still in meditation. Crikey, what a thing to think about after such a peaceful meditation Could this be precognition? After this I fell asleep (I'm sure) ... and I woke up almost on the hour mark. I'll have to speak to Sue/Chris (friends who are mediums) about this one!

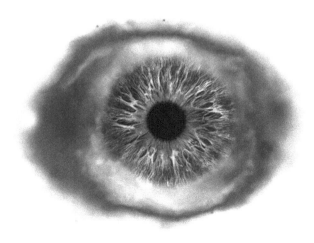

NB 28/1/95 looking back at this people of liberty! AMERICA — That's where the plane crashed. we prelude to the place of the crash!

out of a window. It appeared to be at some sort of large open area, like in the middle of a town centre or city? There was a monument in the centre of my view and people were all walking about, there was a lady pushing a push chair / baby down the front. It was a nice day + the sun was shining ✳ Suddenly I had a weird feeling (thought / picture in my head) whilst looking out of this window. It was of a large plane which was about to crash, it came (or would come) down on its wing after circling in the air. My vision came upon a hole? in the metal somewhere on the body or wing / tail of the plane? It would crash and the figure of '263' came into my head.

The event just disappeared out of my head and I was still in meditation. Crikey, what a thing to think about after such a peaceful scene + what I was looking at before.

(could this be precognition?)

After this I fell asleep I'm sure ... and I woke up almost to the hour mark.

I'll have to speak to Sue / Chris about this one!

✳ 26/6/94 - Picture of plane crash in paper. IDENTICAL TO MY VISION IN MEDITATION on FRIDAY 10TH JUNE.

SPIRITUAL PROOF FOR ME!!

26/6/94

LADY (SPOKE TO
7 PM AIRTIME SAID THE
CRASH HAPPENED APX
2:15 → 2:30 PM.

SPIRIT

WAS QUITE CLOSE 26 TO → 3
PM? OR COULD IT BE A GRID REFERENCE?

X Believed to be pilot
error She said, not a
malfunction. Maybe the hole
I saw (cleft was the insignia
on the tail plane !!

NOT A HOLE
? INSIGNIA on TAIL PLANE?

CHINWICH
PISTOL ROLLS x 2
WESTSIDE
X overlaps

SPREAD (BLACK AREA

NOT A
Soviet ??

Public —

Press officer
Public Info officer →
MASTER SARGENT
BOATRIGHT

0101 / Area code
509 / 247 1212
FAIRCHILD AIR BASE IN USA.

Conclusion: As soon as I saw the news article, it was exactly as I viewed the crash. Upon reflection, the monument I saw must have been the statue of liberty … to show the location as USA. Overall, I agree that some of the finer points may be missing, like the tail insignia of the aircraft (which at first, I thought was a hole) had two large black letters L and A not the 2 black bolts, but for me the predictive validity of this case has a strong correlation. There is even a registration code for this B-52H Stratofortress which is No. 61-0026 … interestingly, the number that came into my head started with a 26! Maybe the number 263 had some other significance I've not thought of yet? That night, I rang the US air base and spoke to a lady who was very forthcoming with info. She said they believed it to be pilot error. May all those who lost their lives rest in peace. God bless to their loved ones too.

FLAMES: The B52 explodes as it hits the ground

Four airmen die in bomber crash

THESE are the final moments in a dramatic accident yesterday at an American air base.

As the B52 bomber crashed and exploded in flames at Fairchild Air Force Base in eastern Washington State, killing all four crew members, it was caught on amateur video and later broadcast throughout the country. The video showed the plane tilt sharply to the left at low altitude before slamming into the ground wing-first. The cause is not known. On Monday four people were killed and 22 wounded at the same base when a former airman ran amok with an automatic rifle.

FINAL SECONDS: The bomber cartwheels to earth

The full report in the US: **https://www.historylink.org/File/8716**

I have also managed to find this harrowing video of the final moments of the B52 …which is exactly as I witnessed it. The full link is below:

https://www.youtube.com/watch?v=7-S_NM--evM&feature=youtu.be)

P.S. I included this original newspaper article above with my dream notes and drawings too … but they do resemble the dead sea scrolls—sorry!

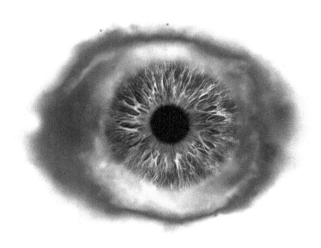

Drowning

Method: Dream—Thursday, 22 December 1994

Time before confirmation/evidence/proof: 6 days—Newspaper article Wednesday, 28 December 1994

Location/landmarks: Roads … then a large open area of water.

People: 6 men

Day or Night: Day/evening/night-time.

Scene: Men struggling to swim.

Colours: None recalled.

Smells: N/A

Vehicles: Car or a cab … then a speedboat.

Feelings: Feeling of dangerous driving/fun in the vehicle. Euphoric … then intense fear in the water.

Dream Log: I already had an earlier dream when suddenly the scene changed again. Someone walked with me, but it wasn't Caroline. A cab pulled up full of friends. The front passenger seat door opens, and I get in and then out again as I've left a cassette tape on the roof. I get out and back in yet again. Everything seems fun … a mass of legs and we're all squashed up.

The cab pulls off and we're on a motorway (?) darting in and out of the cars. I shout, "Bloody hell, that's dangerous!" Very strangely we veer off the road and we're in a speedboat and landed in a large area of water. At this precise point it's as if I'm now watching what's going on from a few yards away.

Hundreds of people were swimming. It felt weird because I couldn't make out what was happening. It looked like a competition. Some people had long 'tubes' over their arms and splashing about (not arm water floats), as if their arms were covered in rubber ... or arms of their jackets filled with water? Nearer to me, people were struggling even more, and yet they seemed to be swimming without tubes or things. People were shouting ... it was euphoric. It felt like a competition, yet the intensity from the people totally didn't fit with what was happening ... as if it was more important than that. Was this a precognitive event—people escaping ... a drowning ... from a ship perhaps? The dream ended.

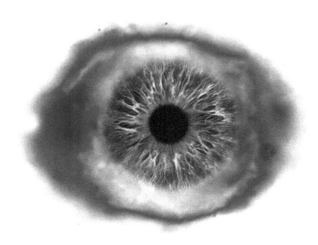

Scene.

Sudden scene change again
Someone walked with me, but it wasn't Caroline
A cab pulled up full of 'friends'. The
front passenger seat door opens and I have got in,
+ then out again ' I've left a cassette on the roof
(TAPE) . I got out and back in again. Everything
seemed 'fun', a mass of legs + were all squashed
up.

The cab pulls off and we're on a motorway
and were darting in and out of the cars. I shout
"Bloody hell, that's dangerous!"

Very strangely we
veer off the road and we're in a speed boat and landed
in a huge area of water.

At this precise point
its as if I'm watching now what's going on from a
few yards away. Hundreds of people were swimming
It felt weird, because I couldn't really make out what
was happening. It looked like a competition? Some
people had long 'tubes' over their arms and splashing
about (not water floats!) as if their arms were covered
in rubber while they struggled to swim.
(or arm of jacket filled with water??)
Nearer to
me, people were struggling even more, yet they seemed to
others, cont

THU 22/12/94   CONT

be swimming without tubes or things... People
were floating — it was euphoric? It felt like
a competition, yet the intensity of the people totally
didn't 'fit' with what was happening — As if it
was not important then that.

PRECOGNITIVE EVENT   —   WAS THIS A
A DROWNING ... A SHIP PERHAPS ??   PEOPLE ESCAPING

The dream ended here.

                                — —

CAB FULL OF (FRIENDS)

ROAD (MOTORWAY?)

A   ♀ ME   ♂ ??

→ MOTORWAY!

CAR

CAB — IN & OUT   DANGEROUS.

6

SPEEDBOAT INTO (WATER)   CONT

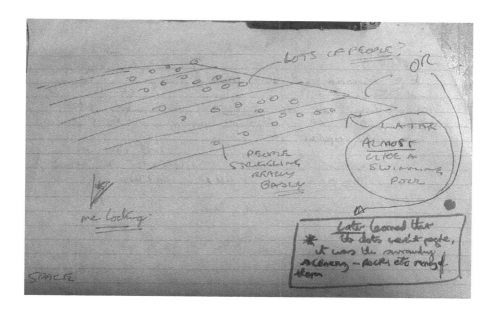

Conclusion: Another tragic event had unfolded before my eyes. Once again, some details seem to be absent, like the colour of the speedboat (which I just found out was red). Bizarre how some of the dream involved the feeling of a competitiveness ... before fear setting in. And why I use the word euphoric ... I'm not sure. Maybe when I wrote the dream notes back in '94, I meant hysteria or panic?

The later image I'd drawn showed up dots in a swimming pool style area of water ... which may have shown the hundreds of people (or the flotilla of local craft) who had been searching for survivors? Yet I also had the feeling that the 'dots' could have somehow indicated scenery? In the water's foreground, I was viewing people struggling really badly. The small drawing in my dream log depicts <u>6</u> people in the speedboat, providing a perfect positive correlation ... and the size of the boat— which turned out to be 19 feet (another report says 20ft)—seems proportionate too.

As I write this, some 28 years later, questions come to mind like … were the 6 friends in a cab going somewhere by road first? (The press stated they had previously gone to a bar). The newspaper 'proof' from Wednesday 28 DECEMBER 1994 and an aerial view of the area are the next two pictures. Notice how the small boats actually look just like dots? Interesting!

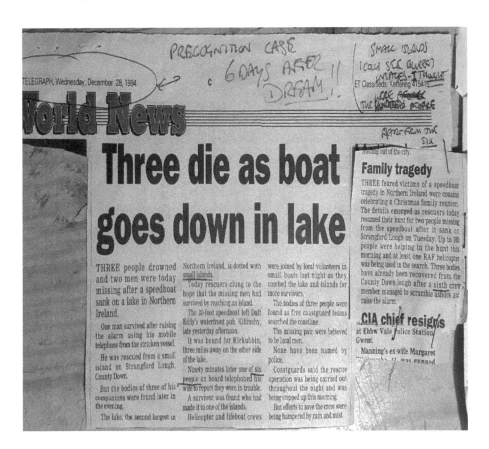

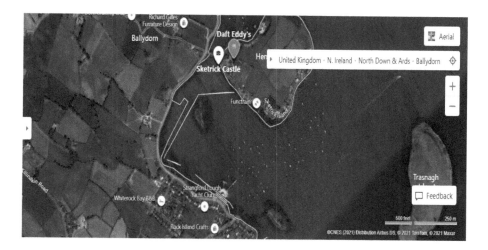

And, because of the internet and today's technology, I have found two online articles from 'The Herald' on the tragedy.

https://www.heraldscotland.com/news/12539008.hopes-fade-for-two-lost-in-speedboat-tragedy-survivor-tells-of-swim-in-the-dark-to-safety-as-friends-drown-after-craft-capsizes/

A very bizarre note in the second article below was the fact the men had apparently turned down the offer of a taxi home only minutes before setting off on their fatal boat journey. It's strange how the taxi-cab details were so prevalent in my dream ... maybe they still used one beforehand to get to the bar? This is the other article, https://www.heraldscotland.com/news/12093465.drowned-men-spent-200-on-drink/   And here's another bizarre thing ... it also states the hull of the speedboat had two 18mm holes drilled in it ... one below the waterline. **Who did this ... and why?**

And I've just found a small additional note where I'd written, 'This was another sad precognitive event, and I've still not experienced/witnessed a 'happy' one yet ... perhaps one day I will. I pray for the families here on the earth-plane, but also know that the spirit world would rejoice because they have returned home!'

On a lighter note (regarding my drawings) ... who would think I had an 'A' grade in O level art? Ghee whizz!

Fire and Water

Method: 2 Dream's—Sunday, 1 January 1995

Time before confirmation/evidence/proof: 8 days—Newspaper Monday, 9 January 1995

Location/landmarks: Sea … coast, beach, large shoreline.

People: Dozens of people running.

Day or Night: Day.

Scene: Horrendous storm, tornado, twister, whirlwind?

Colours: Black, grey/blue/dark, and sandy brown.

Smells: N/A

Vehicles: N/A

Feelings: Panic!

Dream Log: This dream was actually in 2 or 3 parts … or was one long disjointed one. Before I go into the main precognition above, a few things to note had occurred before hand. I had a flash of light and then a multiple lightening burst of light, possibly 4 or 5 sharp peaks. This has occurred at least 4 or 5 times this week, and each time this took place I have been given/shown flames or a fireplace/roaring fire. It was as if a constant reminder of an incident around 'fire.'

One of these instances could have been a precognition because 3 days later there was a massive fire of hay and straw. There was a local tv report I'd watched which had shown hundreds of bales on fire, and they actually looked like the image I drew as part of the night's activity.

The problem here is that I've no newspaper reports and even hours search online (24 DECEMBER 2021) I've found nothing at all to back this up. I have mentioned it here as the dream occurred the same night … and for future reference just in case 'proof' comes to light at a later date. The next one may also be disputed as I have no exact location details … other than what occurred must have affected an area of the world that is subject to horrendous tornadoes and the like.

After I woke up, I had a (this) feeling of America, but I can't prove this, so here goes! There was a scene change within the dream which brought me to a beach, and I was looking at people on the shoreline. Something in the sea, something large and round appeared from nowhere, almost like a huge 'ball' and it was spinning towards them. The ball was black in colour. Weird. The people started to run. They were scared. Could the ball represent a storm, hurricane, tempest?

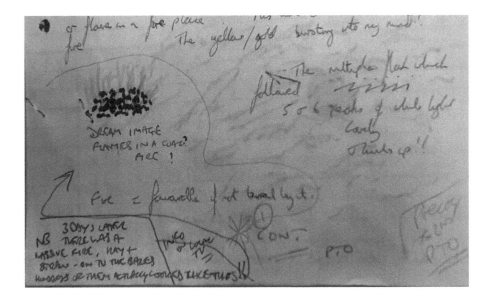

A scene change brought me to a beach and it was as if I was looking at people on the shoreline. Something in the sea, something large travel appeared from nowhere almost like a ~~higher~~ large 'ball' and it was spinning towards them. The ball was black in colour! (weird!) The people start to run. They were scared.

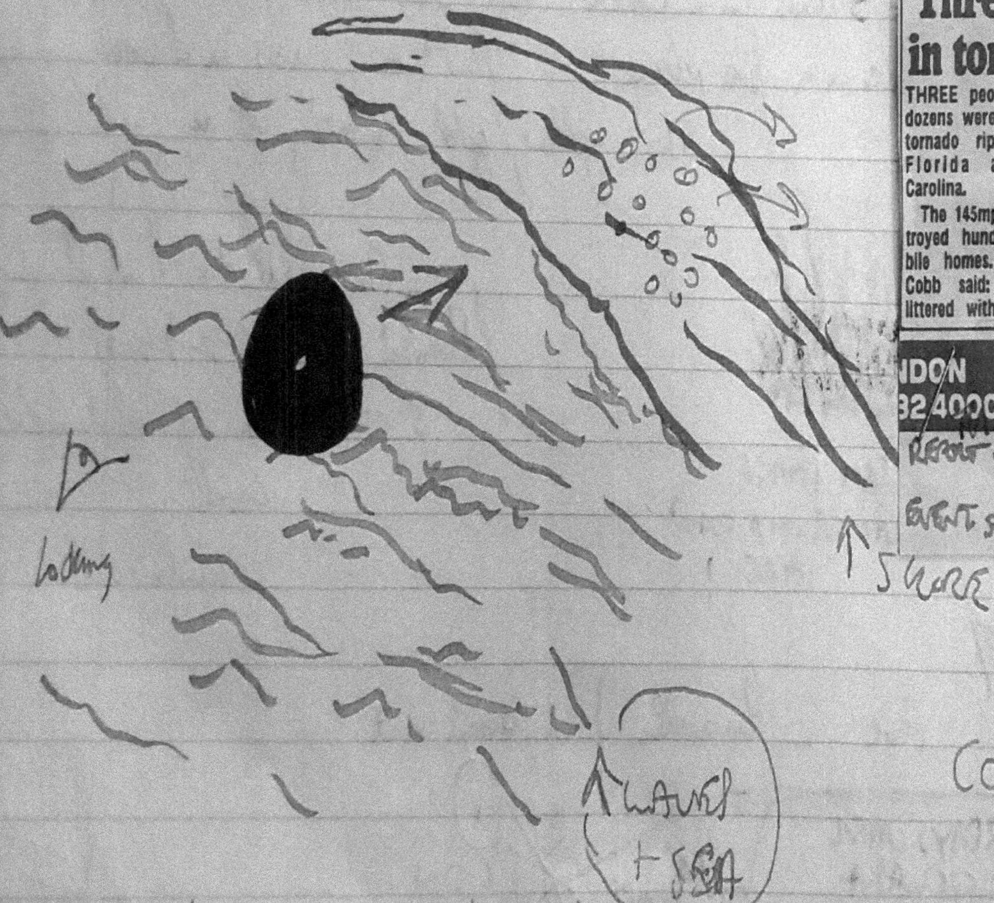

Looking

RECORD MON 9/4/95
EVENT SUN 8/1/95

↑ SHORE

↑ TRAVEL
+ SEA

CONT

Could the ball represent a storm, hurricane?? tempest! PRECOGNITIVE ???

Conclusion: As mentioned above, with the massive fire of hay and straw, I'm struggling to get any hard evidence at all other than on the local television report I must have seen at the time. I'd therefore say this is a weak correlation. It's strange though, that I repeatedly saw fires and flames in my dreams all that week. Perhaps it was the forebode of things soon to come?

Obviously, fires occur all the time, but the following instances, which I've noted, are all quite prominent cases. The very next day on the 2 JANUARY 1995, a fire broke out in Stormont Parliament Buildings in Ireland. There were massive bush fires in Southern Australia from the 4 JANUARY 1995. On the 6 JANUARY 1995, there was a chemical fire in an apartment complex in Manila Philippines, which lead to a discovery of a planned mass-terrorist attack. And yet another fire at the John Dickinson High School in the USA on the 15 JANUARY 1995. More than just coincidences, I'd say!

Now, regarding the weather case ... one small UK based newspaper report mentions a tornado that ripped through Florida and North Carolina. I'd say this has only moderate correlation because I am unfortunately cannot provide more accurate details.

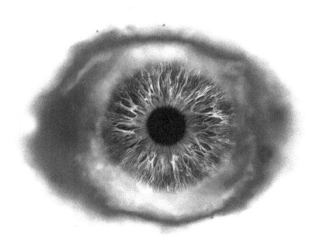

PRECOGNITION 5

Robbers and Escaped Prisoners

Method: 2 x Dreams (seemed to be interlinked)—Monday, 2 January 1995

Time before confirmation/evidence/proof: 1, 3, 6 and 7 days—TV news and newspapers articles

Location/landmarks: Toilet … train station (?), houses, alley/hill, water nearby … river/coast?

People: 6 men (thieves) … then 3 men escaped prisoners.

Day or Night: A sunny day/Night

Scene: 6 men—safecrackers £6,000,000. Toilet-urinals and 3 men running … then resting.

Colours: Black and white. Dark bushes, blue and green empty bottles.

Smells: N/A

Vehicles: Not recalled.

Feelings: Both are crime related. Panic, running-escaping.

Dream Log: I have labelled this precognition 5, but it feels like it should be 5 and 6 as both were linked to crime, but they had their own individual scenes and references. The problem too is that the dreams seemed interlinked … as it was like observing both in the same dream!

I watched on as 6 or 7 men; thieves were talking. (But I may have been the seventh pair of eyes and just viewing). Suddenly an image of a safe … possibly on a wall, I think. They were cracking a safe. The figure of £6,000,000 somehow flashed into me. Something was said about, "Lots of jobs."

The next second, I stood in a toilet. (I say stood but was just there as if 'seeing'). This toilet had 3 or 4 urinals I think, to the right hand side. It may have been in a train station toilet? One man said, "I've had enough. I don't want to go on with this." Someone else then said, "Okay, let's go." Suddenly there was panic … 'police' were coming. Everyone runs away. Some hide. (Everything goes blurry).

2 men run out of the station, and I follow. (3 men). I see them running down an alley between houses. It was like I had tunnel vision as I could only see (or was allowed to see), more or less straight in front of me. Over a stream, up a hill and the 2 men stop for a breather. I passed some bushes. It is a bright sunny day. I notice some empty bottles on the ground. We're together now and looking at a newspaper with a headline '3 names (men) wanted'.

I awoke a second after this and I could not recall the men's names. I wish I could … sorry. It's like they were erased from my memory!

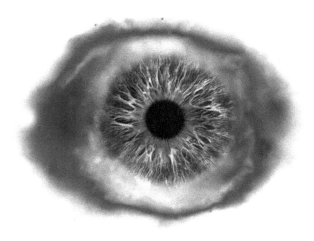

3 × DREAMS:
    1x FLASH IMAGE — A FIRE
                        AGAIN.

1 OF THE DREAMS
            PRECOGNITIVE
"INFORMATION" THAT WOULD BE IN
THE PRESS + on TV. 3 DAYS
            LATER

(NB) — ACTUALLY
        2x
    PRECOGNITION

I begining to think /realise that when I'm
looking upon 'something' in a dream it seems to be
informative or even a precognitive dream, whereas when I'm
actually in the dream ——————— it like I'm being taught
something?

6.49 AM Awoke from the 3rd dream.   Reference the
    above NB
                This 'dream' turned out to be precognitive with
the TV + newspapers producing info 3 days after this dream!!

            THIS IS AN INTERESTING ONE
    (well they all are really but ——————

        I watched as 6 or 7 (was I the seventh?) men
THIEVES were talking. Suddenly an image of a safe
possible on a wall I think — they were cracking a safe
    The figure of £6,000,000 somehow flashed into me.
                            Something was said about "Lots of jobs"
(NB) → 6600000 earlier
        again as in Dream (2)!

SAFE CRACKERS

THIEVES

6 MAYBE 7?

(me)

NB - Dream SPLIT??
2 x PREOCCUPATION?
RON KNIGHT ARTICLE +
3 ESCAPED BORSTAL? PRISONERS
* enough

STATION??

TRACKS
?

The next record I stood in a toilet (I say stood but was just there as if 'seeing') This toilet had 3 (+ urinals I think) to its right hand side. It may have been a TRAIN STATION? TOILET.

One man said, "I've had enough I don't want to go on with this"

Someone else else said, "OKAY, LETS GO"

Suddenly there was panick - 'Police' were coming.

Everyone run away. Some hide. (Everything Blurry really) '2' run out of the station and I follow. I see them running - Down an alley between houses (although it was like I had tunnel vision as if I could only see (or was allowed to see) more or less straight in front of me.

Over a stream, up a hill the 2 men stop for a breather. I passed some bushes, its a bright sunny day, I passed some empty bottles on the ground. Suddenly we're together + we're looking at a newspaper "3 NAMES" "3 NAMES WANTED" ('MEN')

SECOND AFTER THAT, I could not recall the names. I wish I could - surely its like they were erased I can...

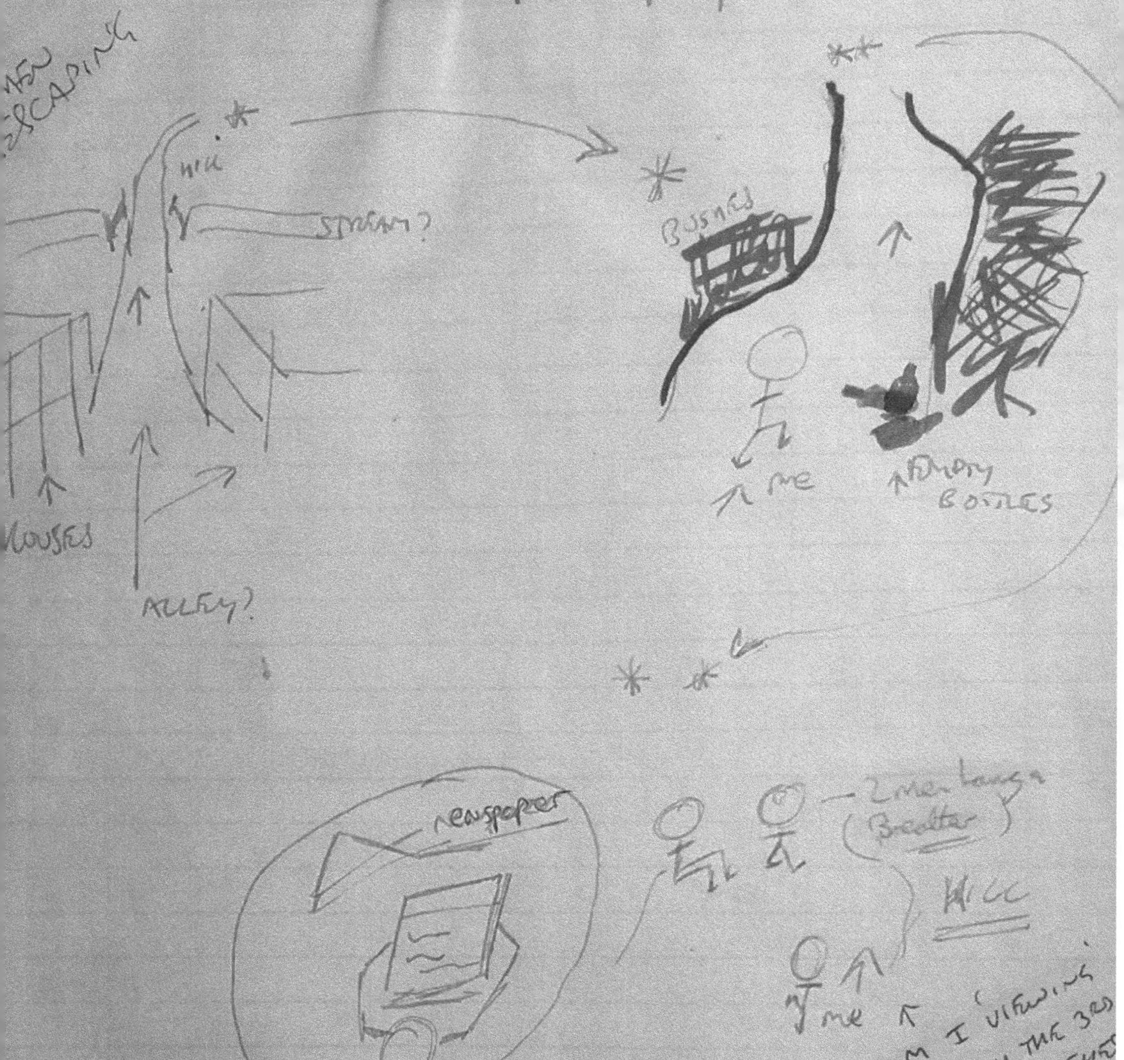

MEN ESCAPING

HILL

STREAM?

HOUSES

ALLEY?

BUSHES

ME

EMPTY BOTTLES

newspaper

2 MEN LONGER (BROTHER)

HILL

ME ↑

AM I VIEWING THROUGH THE 3RD PAIR OF EYES

THURSDAY 6 (7!)
SAFE
£600,000
TOILET
TRAIN STATION
POLICE
PANICK

RUNNING
HOUSES
STREAM
HILL
BUSHES
EMPTY BOTTLES
2 MEN & 3 MEN

NEWSPAPER
NAMES WANTED.

NB. RON KNIGHT, 6 MILL
ARTICLE 3 DAYS
LATER
5/1/95

3 ESCAPED PRISONERS
ARTICLE/EVENT NEXT DAY

+ DIGGER

Maerat
Sea
Water
Country 'WARM' (INDIA??)
DAM.
BARRIER
(DIGGERS
MACHINERY!)

29/12/21 ✻

→ THESE NOTES WERE
LINKED TO A DREAM EARLIER
IN THE NIGHT OF 2/1/95

BUT LOOK AT THE WORDS...
INDIA → INDIAN RESTAURANTS
                                    TOILET?
WATER } REFERENCES TO
SEA   } THE ESCAPED
          PRISONERS LOCATION?

IT'S LIKE EVERYTHING WAS
CONNECTED SOMEHOW!

CONT

THE Sun 22p

Thursday, January 5, 1995   22p   Audited daily sale for November 4,053,274

Betrayed by Ronnie Ratbag

Tricked . . . Barbara always believed Knight was innocent

Marriott . . . lax regime

LAGS ON RUN HAD MASTER KEY TO PRISON

By JAMIE PYATT

PRISON officers warned Parkhurst's governor that lags had a copy of the jail's master key two days BEFORE three killers escaped.

John Marriott was also told that inmates were believed to have stolen jailers' uniforms.

But Prison Officers Association representative Terry McLaren yesterday said nothing was done.

He added: "Officers picked up intelligence that the prisoners may have copies of the keys.

"The governor was informed two days before the escape. We found it extraordinary that direct action was not taken."

Killers Keith Rose, 45, and Andrew Rodger, 64, and self-styled Matthew Williams, 31, were still on the run last night after breaking out of the top-security Isle of Wight jail. The POA's

Continued on Page Two

BABS SLAMS JAILED EX

By IAN HEPBURN and SUE CRAWFORD

EASTENDERS star Barbara Windsor said last night she felt "totally betrayed" by ex-husband Ronnie Knight — jailed over a £6million robbery.

Babs, 57, is furious that

EXCLUSIVE

rat Knight used her name to launder loot from the Security Express raid.

After he got seven years at the Old Bailey, Barbara told The Sun exclusively: "My only

Continued on Page Three

Jail . . . Ronnie Knight

THE FULL AMAZING STORY — PAGES 2, 3, 4 and 5

COP REHEARSED ARREST IN A LOO

THE cop who nailed Knight once stood beside the villain in an Indian restaurant's loo and mentally rehearsed arresting him.

Detective Inspector Reid McGeorge, working undercover, followed Knight into the gents at the crook's curry house in Marbella.

He said: "I wanted to stand next to him so I knew just where I'd put my hand on his shoulder when I nicked him."

Scotsman McGeorge got his chance at Luton airport on May 2 last year, when Knight flew back to face the music. He said: "It was vital to get Knight back to Britain.

"How can you tell your kids crime doesn't pay when there are warrants out in Britain for the arrest of these people and they are living it up on the Costa del -Sol?"

Three more men are still wanted for questioning about the £6million Security Express robbery. They are all living in Spain.

They are Clifford Saxe, 63, a publican from Hackney, East London; Ronald Everitt, 63, an East End property dealer; and John Mason, 62.

Keith Rose . . . cornered by cops

Andrew Rodger . . . on run 5 days

CAPTURED

3 [n]abbed [o]n ferry

Parkhurst . . . three men escaped, [...]

ALL three of the escaped Parkhurst Jail dangermen were recaptured near a ferry port last night.

Killers Keith Rose and Andrew Rodger were dramatically cornered just two minutes after being spotted by off-duty prison officer Mike Jones.

The third escaper, mad bomber Matthew Williams, evaded police and raced off across a darkened field. But he too was tracked down within two hours after scores of officers and dogs closed in on him.

By JAMIE PYATT

Rose, 45, and Rodger, 44, were nabbed just a mile from the harbour at Cowes, on the Isle of Wight's north coast.

Mr Jones saw the trio walking along a road near a roundabout, immediately recognised them and ran to a phone box to raise the alarm.

A dozen police cars screamed to the scene at Whippingham, five miles from

Continued on Page Four

Matthew Williams . . . chased

3 ESCAPED PRISONERS
3/1/95

INFO
1 DAY AFTER PRECOGNITION

ps
economic

Industry
okesman
ernment
labour is
not that
are the

director
Internat-
ritain of

Mail on Sunday's exposure of labour abuses by suppliers to High Street giants

yesterday the Prime Minister what steps are being taken to

Mr Griffiths is taking his protest to Foreign Sec-

Committee, favours economic threats to help

See Human Tragedy: Pages 37-39

MISSING UNIFORMS WARNING GIVEN DAYS BEFORE BREAKOUT

Jail chiefs ignored crucial escape clue

By CHRISTOPHER LEAKE and RICHARD HOLLIDAY

PARKHURST managers knew that three prison officers' uniforms were *missing four days* before a trio of dangerous 'lifers' escaped, it was claimed last night.

Investigators at the Isle of Wight top security jail were also checking claims that no roll-call of inmates was taken after a keep-fit session from which the three vanished.

And it became clear last night that nail-bomber Matthew Williams, 25, and murderers Keith Rose, 45, and Andrew Rodger, 44, may have reached the mainland less than *two hours* after fleeing.

Crossing

Police revealed yesterday that they had been seen crossing the main road past the prison at 7pm on Tuesday — 90 minutes before the search for them was launched and in good time for an 8pm ferry to Portsmouth.

Police also released the descriptions of two possible getaway vehicles. One was a red Ford Escort parked on Monday in an estate off the main road. It disappeared around 7pm on Tuesday.

The second was a Transit-type van with tinted windows, seen parked on Horsebridge Hill

around the time of the escape. Chief Superintendant David Bason, in charge of the hunt, said: 'From what we now know it is quite possible they reached the mainland in one of these vehicles quite quickly.'

He said if the men were still on the island 'someone is feeding them, getting supplies'.

But yesterday the island search was significantly scaled down from 200 officers to only 75.

The first draft inquiry into the escape by the Prison Service's Director of Security, Richard Tilt, will be on Home Secretary Michael Howard's desk tomorrow.

But yesterday Mr Howard turned on the Prison Officers' Association, led by John Bartell, for allowing its Parkhurst members to give only written evidence to the inquiry. He regards the POA's refusal to give verbal evidence as 'outrageous', because it will delay the new security measures.

Mr Howard, who will make a statement to the Commons on Tuesday, said: 'We are determined to get to the bottom of what went wrong. That is why it is so important that everybody fully co-operates with the inquiry.'

He said it was likely that the investigation — and another at Everthorpe, the scene of two riots last week — would lead to new security rules at all prisons.

Opinion — Page 28

A bride's best friend

World News

Briefly...

Two attacked

TWO 23-year-old men are recovering in hospital after a masked gang attacked them with baseball bats in Belfast. Royal Ulster Constabulary sources said they believed the assaults were "so-called punishment beatings". Eight masked men attacked the men late last night on a street in the mainly nationalist area of Ardoyne, north Belfast. The victims sustained broken bones in their arms and hands.

Russians advance

FIERCE fighting engulfed the streets of the Chechen capital Grozny today as Russian troops battled towards the presidential palace. Artillery blasts caused heavy damage to residential areas of the city. And two columns of Russian troops were said to be advancing block by block to within several hundred yards of the blackened palace.

Blow for royals

THE Royal family was rocked by two new polls today which forecast it could be doomed. One survey suggested the Royals would not survive the next 50 years. Half the people quizzed believed the Royal family would die out within the next half century. The poll in today's Guardian showed that although just 28 per cent wanted to abolish the monarchy, while another 34 per cent said they were "not especially keen" on it.

West case bid

THE Crown Prosecution Service was today under fresh pressure to drop murder charges against Rose West after lurid newspaper revelations. The wife of alleged the murder charges. But her solicitor aimed that the chances of her getting a ir trial had been scuppered by nsational stories in two of yesterday's nday tabloids. Fred West was found anged in his prison cell on New Year's ay.

Company gloom

ECONOMIC recovery has failed to boost ausiness confidence, a property market survey revealed today. Most firms were gloomy about their expansion prospects – and nearly a third said they were looking or smaller premises. The main growth area is expected to come from retailers with 48 per cent planning to expand floor space, according to the CBI/Grimley JR Eve poll of 329 firms.

Nanny guide

. LEAFLET offering guidance on mploying nannies has been published by ne Metropolitan Police. Det Sgt Wendy Iilton, of Scotland Yard, who is a new um herself, came up with the idea after ealing with a disturbing baby battering se.

loor collapse

HREE staff are recovering today after ading in a heap in a pub cellar when the or collapsed beneath them. The three ffered cuts and bruises after falling 10 t through the floor at the Queen's pub in kenhead, Merseyside.

■ AT BAY . . . the scene on the Isle of Wight as police closed in on the Parkhurst escapers

Escapers planned to flee by plane

ALL three Parkhurst Prison escapers are back behind bars.

The three men were caught after five days on the run on the Isle of Wight after being spotted by prison officers on their way to work at Parkhurst.

Murderers Keith Rose, 44, and Andrew Rodger, 44, were cornered by police less than a mile from the Cowes ferry terminal soon after 7pm last night.

The third man, explosives __ _ _illiams, 25, was caught two hours later trying to swim to freedom in a river two miles north of where the other two were caught.

The dangerous trio confirmed they had tried to steal a plane to escape the Isle of Wight. Rose is a qualified pilot.

But they told Parkhurst's Board of Visitors chairman Richard Gully they could not start the Cessna aircraft at the island's Sandown Airport.

The men were finally spotted by off-duty Parkhurst prison warders Colin Jones and Grant Ford – who were on their way to work – near a roundabout six miles from the jail at 7.10pm yesterday.

Mr Jones raised the alarm immediately while his colleague kept a close watch on the dangerous trio.

More than a dozen police cars and vans arrived at the scene in seconds. The first three officers to arrive arrested Rose and Rodg without a struggle.

Officers gave chase aft Williams was reported to ha dived through a hedge alongsid nearby racecourse, leaving jacket behind.

Warder Grant Ford said: "T looked completely whacked, Williams had enough left in hir run off as soon as he realised t had been spotted."

An exhausted Williams la gave himself up after tryin swim for freedom in a river.

Police saw the arrests vindication of their convicti that the men had remained on island.

Bonzo gets his man...

A POLICE dog handler plunged up to his neck in a river to arrest dangerous jailbreak fugitive Matthew Williams.

PC Tony Woolcock spotted the escaped convict and immediately gave chase with his dog Bonzo – even though Williams dived into the River Medina.

PC Woolcock said: "We chased him and he jumped into the water. I jumped in after him and detained him. I went in up to my neck. He wasn't offering resistance."

The 41-year-old officer, who is normally based in the New Forest, said he did not give a thought to his own safety.

He said: "I didn't think about it at all. I was just wet."

Hampshire Assistant Chief Constable Peter Linden Jones said: "We had no positive sightings of them on the mainland. Therefore we had to assume they were still here."

Hampshire Chief Constable John Hoddinott said he was considering recommending some officers and warders for bravery awards.

He said: "This is a triumph for perseverance and old fashioned coppering of which I am very much in favour."

■ HERO . . . Grant Ford, who kept a watch on the escapers while a c-ll---

Parkhurst . . . three men escaped, but were back behind bars last night

CAPTURED

Continued from Page One
the jail. The first three officers to arrive arrested Rose and Rodger without any struggle.

The prisoners were bundled into separate police vans and taken back to Parkhurst, where they will later be questioned about their five days on the run.

It is believed police searching roads and fields found an insecure shed, which may have been the hideout used by the trio as they made their way towards the terminal at Cowes.

Ferries and hydrofoils provide a fast service from there to Southampton.

Rose and Rodger were caught just after 7pm. Williams was apprehended two hours later.

As police closed in on him, an urgent radio alert was flashed to ferry staff at Fishbourne, another port about three miles away.

Police found Williams' jacket, which he threw off as he dived through a hedge beside a race-course north of Whippingham.

A caravan park bor-dering the track was sealed off by armed officers, one of whom said that it was now believed Williams was wearing glasses as a disguise.

Police with tracker dogs poured into the area as a spotter plane equipped with a thermal imaging heat-seeking camera swooped low overhead.

Just before he was caught, one officer said: "It will only be a matter of time before we find where he is hiding.

"Once he reaches the water's edge, there is nowhere else for him to go."

Police, desperate to avoid a hostage stand-off, had warned all residents to stay in their homes and lock all doors and windows.

Local John Gaudion, 44, barred himself and his family in as the hunt went on right outside his home.

Mr Gaudion said: "It is frightening and we hve been told to stay inside.

"There are loads of flashing lights outside and police in flak jack-ets. There is an aircraft overhead — all hell ha broken loose."

Barmaid Kelly Barker 19, told how she drove into police as they se up roadblocks on the remote Whippingham to East Cowes road.

Kelly, who was on her way to work at the Folly Inn pub a Whippingham, said: "I was terrifying. Dozens of police appeared from nowhere. Five vans full of officers raced pas me and pulled up sud denly in front.

"The police jumped out and started search ing the woods and fields."

Last night news o the men's capture wa relayed to relatives o some of their victims who had been under police guard since they escaped. A number had received death threats.

Keith Rose's mothe Joyce Tippett was "very relieved" her son had been caught because she had feared police would kill him in a shootout.

Rose's stepfather John Tippett said at home in Exeter, Devon: "She has been worried sick."

Closing in . . police combed every part of the Isle of Wight in hunt for tri

I'LL HAVE TO ESCAPE—Page 13

Conclusion: It's quite bizarre how these crime stories seem to merge into one. And, upon investigation, the Security Express HQ robbery (Great Train Robbery) involved a 9 man gang …so the 6 men in one segment of the dream plus 3 men in another dream reference adds up.

Then there's the precise information like the £6 million pounds and even a feeling of a hot climate–with India coming to mind in my dream log–now looks more than a tenuous link to the toilets in the Indian restaurant in Marbella … where the detective had imagined he'd be arresting Ronnie Knight! The way the dreams panned out makes me feel its predictive validity has a strong correlation.

However, the feeling of panic and running/hiding with the presence of water nearby was so powerful (for the 3 men 'escaping' precognition) that this implies they were separate. The little sketch of what I thought looked like a station (especially the roof with pillars) looks remarkably like the last photo in this sequence. Perhaps you can decide yourself from the dream log and the news articles which I've kept since 1995.

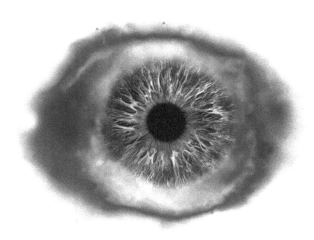

Train Crash

Method: Flashes proceeding a dream—Tuesday 31 January 1995

Time before confirmation/evidence/proof: 1 day— TV News + the subsequent internet articles found in 2021.

Location/landmarks: Train station, newspaper stall, carriages

People: Newspaper stall holder, Train conductor, lots of people moving in one direction.

Day or Night: Night.

Scene: Train not moving … people moving left to right.

Colours: Black and white, White to red, and dark red colour.

Smells: N/A

Vehicles: Trains. Also, symbolism of a 'fast' train.

Feelings: Urgency … hearing loud impact/pop/bang/explosion.

Dream Log: I began to run …I found myself in a train station. Someone (or two people) … a man and a lady who were with me run onto a train. I run over towards a newspaper stand, on the floor were magazines and papers. I started to pick them up and search for a newspaper rather hurriedly. A man says, "What are you doing?" I reply: 'I've got to have todays newspaper'.

Obviously, he never had it and I found myself running up to a train which was stationary. A lot of people seemed to move further down the platform to get on the train. It was about to leave. I hammered on the window of the carriage where I saw someone get in. A conductor—a fairly old man—with a cap came to the window. I said, 'Let me on. I've got to get on and I need your newspaper'.

At first, he was directing me away, but I persisted, and I suddenly found myself on the train which started to move, and I began walking down the aisle reading a newspaper. There seemed to be a pause and then a large bang. This actually sounded like a loud pop to me ... but also like an explosion? My mind seemed blank but then I began to shout at someone (?) who I didn't (or couldn't) see. 'Why, why, why did you do it?' There was no reply.

There was another split second pause and suddenly a picture of circles formed in my mind. The colour red (I think) filling these circles which were sort of interconnected themselves. (Picture to follow). Then I found myself looking back on what looked like the front of a huge train (?) but almost resembling the cone/cockpit of a plane. It was quite dark around it, as if it stuck out of a platform or tunnel. The colour was dark red, and it has a white flash down the side. I then woke up at 4.38 a.m.

Was this (a type of train) in the far east ... Japan or China? I lay awake for an age, an hour perhaps, and then started to cry. I felt so completely in touch with 'spirit'. It was amazing to feel as 'one'. I don't know (at least so far) whether there would be any casualties in this future event. That is always sad ... but if it is karmic perhaps it is meant to be. How can I truly describe how this all feels, as words cannot convey? But I do feel privileged and blessed that 'spirit' is using me (not ego) and trusts me. Thank you.

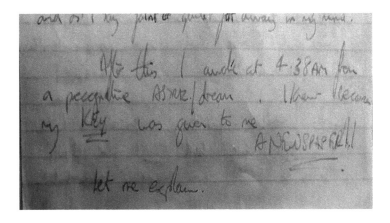

DREAM NOTES?

I began to run — I found myself on a train station — someone or two people a man + lady who 'were' with me ran on to catch a train.

I run towards a newspaper stand — on the floor were magazines & papers ... I started to pick and search for a newspaper rather hurriedly

"What are you doing?!" Me → "I've got to have TODAY'S newspaper."

Obviously he never had it — I found myself running up to a train — which was stationary. A lot of people seemed to move further down the platform to get on the train — it was about to leave.

I hammered on the window of the carriage where I saw someone get in. A conductor — a fairly old man with a cap came to the window. "Let me on, I've got to get on — + I need your newspaper."

At first he was directing me away, but I persisted + I suddenly found myself on the train, which started to move and I began walking down the aisle reading a newspaper.

There seemed a pause and then a large bang. This actually sounded (to me) like a loud POP! but it was like an explosion. My mind seemed blank but

CONT

TUESDAY 21/1/95 cont:

I began to shout at someone(?) who I didn't
(or can't) see

"Why!?! Why! did you do it?"

There was no reply.

There was another
split second pause and then suddenly a picture
of circles formed in my mind — There was a
colour "red" (I think) filling these circles which
were sort of interconnected in themselves.
(Picture to follow).

Suddenly I found myself
looking back at what looked like the front of a
huge train (?) but almost like the nose / cockpit of a
plane. It was quite dark all around it — As
if it stuck out a platform or tunnel. The
colour was dark red and it had a white flash
down the side.

I then woke up!

Was this in the far east — Japan? (or china?)

I lay awake for an age, 1 hour?
I started to cry — I felt so completely in tune
with Spirit — it was amazing to feel as one.
I don't think or at least I didn't know whether
there would be any consulting in the future ever?
— that is always said — but if it is KARMIC its meant
to be. How can I truly describe how it feels?
Words cannot. I feel privileged, and blessed that
Spirit is using me (not ego ego) and trusts me. Thank

so much Spirit.

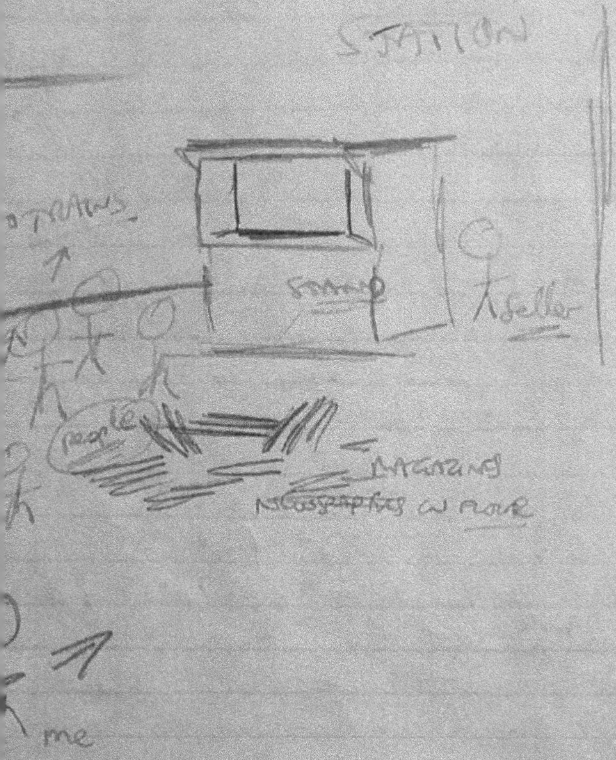

STATION

TRAINS

STAND

seller

people

MAGAZINES

NEWSPAPERS ON FLOOR

me

CONDUCTOR

TRAIN

me "Please, I must get on
I need the (your) newspaper!"

PEOPLE   ALL THE
THIS WAY

The circles.

The colour seemed
to start to fill
the circles.

Could this be
blood ??

Could the circles repeat
people — people hurt ??

My first
impression was circles of Olympic games but there
turned to be more than 5 I'm sure.

Picture of van outside of it my last image.

Or could it
be a
plane?!
cockpit

✓ THIS
SEEMED
HUGE.

12:11 🌐 14˚ ✉ •   🔕 🛜 ᵛᵒⁱⁱ ⊪ 87% ▪

✕   🔒 **Accident at Ais Gill...**   ⬜   ⬐   ⋮
          railwaysarchive.co.uk

You are in RA » Accident Archive » Accident at Ais Gill on 31st
January 1995

Accident at Ais Gill on 31st January 1995

Accident Summary

Location
Ais Gill

Train Operator
British Rail (Provincial)

Primary Cause
Landslip

Secondary Cause
Inadequate communication

Result
Derailment, head on collision

1 fatality, 30 injured

Accident Investigation Status
This accident has been the subject
of a published formal accident
investigation, which you will find
below.

View our accidents map

View location in Rail Map Online »

Please note that the Railways Archive is not responsible
for the content of external websites

Wikipedia article »

Please note that the Railways Archive is not responsible
for the content of external websites. **The accuracy of
Wikipedia articles should not be taken for granted.**

Related Documents

Link [?]	Document	Date
	Railway Accident Near Ais Gill: A Report on the Fatal Accident that occurred on 31 January 1995 near Ais Gill, on the line from Carlisle to Leeds in t...	Oct 1997

Related News Stories

There are currently no news items related to this

||| ◯   ‹

The 1995 Ais Gill rail accident occurred near Ais Gill, Cumbria, UK, at about **18:55 hrs** on 31 JANUARY 1995 when a class 156 Super-Sprinter was derailed by a landslide on the Settle-Carlisle Railway line and was subsequently run into by a similar train travelling in the opposite direction. The Guard of the first train was fatally injured in the collision.

1995 Ais Gill rail accident

For the accident in 1913, see 1913 Ais Gill rail accident.

Ais Gill rail accident (1995)	
Details	
Date	31 January 1995 18:55
Location	Aisgill, Cumbria
Country	England
Line	Settle-Carlisle Line
Cause	Line obstructed by landslide
Statistics	
Trains	2
Deaths	1
Injured	30+
List of UK rail accidents by year	

Actual Event: A Class 156 Super-Sprinter formed the 1626 Carlisle to Leeds via Settle service (headcode 2H88). It could only proceed as far as Ribblehead railway station, about 12 miles north of Settle, as the lines from Ribblehead to Settle were blocked by flooding; so it had to return to Carlisle. The driver changed cabs as the train was now heading northbound instead of southbound and proceeded back over the Ribblehead Viaduct and on to Aisgill Summit, the highest point on the line at 1,169 feet (356 m) above sea level. It was dark and raining heavily.

Near Aisgill Summit itself the train hit a landslide. It derailed across both tracks, and the cabin lights went off. The injured driver managed to radio Crewe Control Room. The conductor escorted passengers into the rear unit, which was across the northbound track. He then returned to see the driver who was still in the cab. Either the conductor or the driver (it is not known which) changed the lights from white to red to warn oncoming trains of the obstruction but no other action was taken.

Meanwhile, another Super-Sprinter train forming the 1745 Carlisle to Leeds service (headcode 2H92) had set off from Kirkby Stephen railway station around five miles to the north. About a quarter of a mile before the derailed train, the driver saw its red lights and made an emergency brake application, but there was no chance of stopping before impacting the derailment. The collision killed the conductor of the derailed train, and seriously hurt several passengers: 30 people on the trains suffered some kind of injury. The signalman at Settle Junction signal box was informed of the accident by the conductor of the 2H92 service and the emergency services were then alerted.

Inquiry:

The official inquiry concluded that the conductor of 2H88 failed in his paramount duty to protect his train in the event of an incident by laying down detonators and displaying a red flag one mile from the obstruction. The time between the initial derailment and the subsequent collision was about six or seven minutes which would have allowed a much greater warning time to be given to the second train and might have prevented the collision or at least reduced its impact. The inquiry noted that a transcript of the call made from the driver of the train that hit the landslide. In his communications with the control centre at Crewe, the call ended with a control saying, "we will take care of all of that, driver." This may have given the false impression that the southbound service that hit the first stricken service, would be warned appropriately and so the guard set about tending to the needs of his passengers. The chairman of the inquiry, Mr E N Clarke, said that protecting the train should have been the priority of the guard.

Further recommendations were made concerning the inadequate communications between Railtrack Control Rooms and inefficient use of the National Radio Network. A "group call" to all trains in the vicinity of the incident could have been made by the Control Room and might have alerted the second train to the obstruction in time to prevent the collision.

Here is another article, Guards death could have been avoided:

https://web.archive.org/web/20170202044550/
http://www.cwherald.com/a/archive/guard-s-death-could-have-been-avoided.234637.html

Conclusion: It seems that this event occurred literally hours after my dream! Now, as I look at my drawings from all those years ago and the front of the train, it clearly isn't from 1995! I have checked online and can't find any trains or even the front of a plane that resembles it. The picture inset into the screen shot shows carriages which look very similar to my earlier drawing though. The red colour could simply represent the real danger involved, or even blood/death? Also, red in the circles (which initially made me think of the Olympic rings is very bizarre), and might represent the lanterns/lights that were being switched from white to red?

Such discrepancies may well give me much lower predictive validity on this event, but the facts show there was a major collision, (the loud bang/pop/explosion) and a single fatality … the poor conductor/guard who I drew inside the carriage. He bravely helped to save a large group of people by moving them to another carriage/ further towards the back of the train, just like the arrows on the drawing itself, too.

Overall, there are some striking similarities. However, because of the separate red train (?) which was so vivid and unique (which could be from a completely different future event), it's only fair to say this is a moderate correlation. You might think that's harsh, but remember, I wasn't aware of any landmarks or the severe weather conditions either.

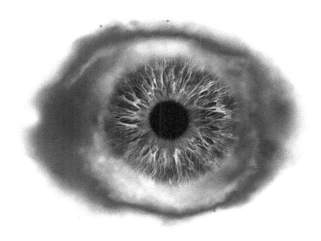

PRECOGNITION 7

Football Violence/Stabbing

Method: Dream—Friday, 7 April 1995

Time before confirmation/evidence/proof: 1 day—Newspaper/Internet articles found in 2021.

Location/landmarks: Street, Pub.

People: A lot of men. A man with a knife.

Day or Night: Day.

Scene: Terrible violence … people/men fighting.

Colours: Red and Black. Blue lights.

Smells: N/A

Vehicles: Van/coach.

Feelings: Anger/hatred.

Dream Log: Precognition. (An overview—Outside shop (in fact a Pub). A van – large (in fact a coach). Fans fighting—terrible violence. Police about … and I'm asked to help identify the murderer. I have a vision of someone wearing a red and black jacket – Man Utd?)

Everything seemed to be misting over and then became clear. It was as if I was opposite a shop in a street. A van(?) was parked opposite a large window and slightly to the left of me. Then a 'feeling' of danger—not for me—but at what was going on 'came over me'.

Suddenly there were men (football fans) fighting and a few of them had remarkably similar hairstyles, sort of curly to collar length style. A man in a small group lunged forward and seemed to catch another in his neck … a knife wound, I think. After another couple of seconds everybody dispersed and ran in different directions. Police arrived and I could see blue flashing lights in the background.

There seemed another pause and then two figures walked in front of my vision, and I took these for policemen. A lady walked up to the window (which I was behind again) and said, "Who can help here? Can any of you help with this?" At this point I again felt 2 or 3 people to my left and everyone said no by shrugging their shoulders. She looked at me and I didn't reply. "Come on!" she said, "One of you must have seen something! There has been a murder, and someone must be able to help!" (NB. I'm still in dream state remember).

I nodded to say, 'I can help' and suddenly what I had seen/witnessed a few moments earlier started to 'replay' as if in a video. IE. The men fighting. As this went on, the video then stopped, and my vision seemed to go blurred. In this dream 'state' I then asked 'spirit' could I see this again. Suddenly it did!

My vision 'zoomed' in towards two men, one in a grey jacket and shirt and another in sort of a patterned top. The person who was hit in the neck, I'm sure had blonde hair. As this stopped—I began to think … but the man didn't look as if he was murdered … he ran away, I'm sure? A second passed and an image of a man—standing next to the van appeared. He looked like this. (See drawing in original dream log further below … squiggly dark hair wearing a red and black chequered shirt or jacket). As soon as he caught my eye/my vision, everything … including him, disappeared! Was he the murderer or murdered man?

FOOTBALL STADIUM + KILLING
MATCH 100/0 ①
YES PREFEC- NITION
FRIDAY NIGHT
7/4/95
③ × DREAMS — ASTRAL (PRECOGNITION?) × 13
— CONFIRMED SUN 9/4/95 (ON TV)

I feel that all 3 were of a sequence — connected by one thing of which I'll explain. It seemed that I had astralled and at one part I may I have an indication of where Spirit wishes me to work in the future.

Everything seemed to be misting and then it become clear.
It was as if I was opposite a shop in a street. A van? was parked opposite the window and slightly to the left of me.
Then a 'feeling of danger — not for me but at what was going on 'came over me.'
Cont

THIS IS WHAT WAS A COACH!

(2)

THIS TURNS OUT TO BE A PUB

VAN?

SHOP?

RUNNING

Men FIGHTING

RUNNING

Suddenly there were men (football fans?) fighting and a few of them had very similar hair styles — short sort of curly to collar to length — style

↑ me looking ↑

A man in a small group lunged forward and reached to catch another on his neck — a knife wound I think.

After another couple of seconds everybody dispersed + ran in different directions. Police had arrived and I could see blue flashing lights in the the background.

There reared another pause and then 2 figures walked in front of my van (and I took these for policemen.) A lady walked up to the window (which I was behind again!) and said "Who can help here? — can any of you help with this?"

At this point I again felt 2/3 people to my left and everyone round me by shrugging their shoulders. She looked at me and I didn't reply

"Come on!" she said "One of you must have seen something! There has been a murder and someone must be able to help!"

(NB REMEMBER I'M STILL IN DREAM STATE WILL REMEMBER) I nodded to say, 'I can help' and suddenly what I had seen/witnessed a few moments earlier started to 'replay' as if on a video. ie The men fighting.

My vision 'zoomed in' to two men one in a grey jacket + shirt and another sort of a patterned top. The person who was hit in the neck I'm sure had blonde hair.

As this went on then, it stopped and my vision resorted to go blurred. In this dream 'State', I then asked Spirit could I see this again. Suddenly it did!!

As this then stopped - I began to think - but the man didn't look as if he was murdered ... he ran away I'm sure?

A second passed and a image of a man - standing next to the car appeared. He looked like this →

— STRAGGLY DARK HAIR

— RED + BLACK CHECKED SHIRT OR JACKET

As soon as he caught my eye /my vision, everything, including him disappeared!

— WAS HE THE MURDERER OR MURDERED ??
— MAN

*

I DIDN'T REALISE AT THE TIME MAN UTD COLOURS !! 'IE SYMBOLIC'

(CONT//

The silver F-reg Vauxhall Astra

Three arrests after fan dies

THREE football fans have been arrested after a man died in a clash between Manchester United and Crystal Palace supporters before the FA Cup semi-final clash at Villa Park.

The man died after fighting flared outside a pub in Walsall pub less than an hour before the kick off.

Another fan, a man in his 30s, was fighting for his life today with serious head injuries.

bring it back the way they took it.

"Don't do this to Kye. It isn't fair."

The fighting left four other fans needing hospital treatment.

Police have not yet named the dead man, who was 35 and from Surrey.

The two sets of supporters had stopped off for a lunchtime drink at the New Fullbrook Pub, Walsall, five miles from the ground.

Witnesses said that as the fans left the pub to go to the game, the Manchester United supporters attacked

to pay for the out-of-date term, from September to Christmas.

the Palace coach. They hurled bricks, stones and bottles and a series of vicious fights broke out.

The tragedy has been blamed on ill feeling between fans which has simmered since January when United star Eric Cantona attacked Palace supporter Matthew Simmons following his sending off at Selhurst Park.

● Match report – see Sport on Monday, page 8

Join us on a trip to the beautiful

PRECOGNITION CASE

2 FREE TICKETS T...
TOKEN 1 ON PAGE 13

CUP THUGS KILL FAN

United mob attack in Cantona flare-up

EXCLUSIVE: SUN MAN SHARES £2.7M JACKPOT

I want you Lott to be my family

PAUL CAN AFFORD TO ADOPT HIS STEPKIDS

EXCLUSIVE by
DAVID WOODING

JUBILANT Lottery winner Paul Titchmarsh hugged his wife's three kids yesterday and told them: "Now I can afford to become your dad."

Sun reader Paul was in a syndicate which scooped a £2.7million slice of Saturday's £9million jackpot.

Paul's share is a whopping £877,000.

That's enough to rake in £1,000 a week interest if he decides to invest it and watch it grow.

But Paul is going to dip into his pot to put his family first.

The caring dad plans to

Continued on Page Seven

Dad'll do nicely... Paul and Tina with the kids   Picture: SIMON BUNTING

By **ANDREW PARKER**

A SOCCER fan was murdered yesterday in a grudge battle over banned Eric Cantona.

Another supporter was stabbed as taunts about the United star exploded into mayhem.

Fighting erupted as two

coachloads of Manchester United and Crystal Palace fans piled out of the same pub just before the FA Cup semi-final. The dead man was believed to a 35-year-old dad of four from Surrey.

United fans screamed "Ooh, ah Cantona" to taunt their rivals over the Frenchman's kung-fu tack on a Palace fan. Horrified

Continued on Page Two

WHY I'M RETIRING, BY ROD STEWART
BIZARRE SPECIAL PAGES 16 & 17

CUP FAN KILLED

Continued from Page One

families in nearby houses houses watched as the Palace coach was pelted with bricks and bottles — then 100 fans waded into each other with fists, boots and knives.

The man who died was kicked and battered to the ground by several attackers.

Another suffered serious stab wounds and was in critical condition in hospital last night. Another four were hurt.

Police raced to the car park of the New Fullbrook pub in Walsall, West Midlands, at 2.30pm — 90 minutes before the kick-off at Birmingham's Villa Park five miles away.

Onlooker Hilda O'Sullivan, 65, said: "There were people running all over the road. One lad lay soaked in blood not moving."

Ronald Mellor, 26, said: "The United fans were going mad. It was carnage." Police are trying establish how the fans arrived at the same place despite plans to bring buses off the M6 at different exits.

Match report — Pages 30-31

British Universities
Film & Video Council
moving image and sound, knowledge and access

LEARNING
ON SCREEN

About Learning on Screen   Contact Us   Sign in

adio   Events   Moving Image Gateway   News on Screen   Archives & Footage   Shakespeare   Find DVDs   Copyright Guidance

ch

LBC

rch

search

(LBC/IRN)

cords

is violence and

Records

Football fans violence and death

Mark or unmark the record
About marked records »

How to cite this record   ▸

Title	Football fans violence and death
Genre	Interview
TX Date	10 Apr 1995
Year of production	1995
Play audio	To listen to the audio files, please log in .
Duration	00:02:08
Description	Bruce Whitfield interviews Superintendent David Claydon of the West Midlands Police on the incident in which Crystal Palace fan Paul Nixon died and four others were injured in pre-match violence in Walsall, Birmingham, in a pub car park shortly before the semi-final championship match between Manchester United and Crystal Palace this afternoon.
Contributors	Bruce Whitfield ; David Claydon
Keywords	Deaths , Association football , Birmingham , Hooliganism , Manchester United , Walsall , Crystal Palace (football team) , Paul Nixon

Record Stats

This record has been viewed 457 times.

11:53  •   84%

Menu ≡

Wednesday 12th April 1995

Crystal Palace 0-2 Manchester United

FA Cup Semi Final Replay – Att: 17,987

Manager: Alan Smith

Crystal Palace fans boycotted the FA Cup Semi Final Replay due to the events that led to the death of Paul Nixon just three days earlier. Under 18,000 people turned up to Villa Park to witness United's progression to the final:

"We sincerely believe the match should not be played so soon after the dreadful events of last Sunday," Colin Noades said, *"and we are anxious to avoid any further serious incidents.*

"This was the third serious instance of appalling behaviour at games involving the two clubs. Two years ago at Selhurst Park, a Crystal Palace supporter received multiple stab wounds minute's a match against Manchester United.

"Earlier this year we saw the Eric Cantona

Menu ≡

"Earlier this year we saw the Eric Cantona incident, then last Sunday. It is long overdue for Manchester United to make a statement concerning their supporters' activities, and to take the necessary action."

A minutes silence was held before kick-off in memory of Paul Nixon (pictured above).

Nigel Martyn had broken his finger in the first match and was missing from the game that, quite frankly, the Palace players could not get themselves up for. Steve Bruce (29) opened the scoring, taking advantage of his regular marker Iain Dowie being off the field to replace a contact lens, and Gary Pallister (40) gave United a 2-0 lead at half time.

Seven minutes into the second half Roy Keane received his first red card in English football – for stamping on Gareth Southgate. Unfortunately, Darren Patterson also received his marching orders for his involvement in the ensuing melee.

Team Line-ups

1 Peter Schmeichel	1 Rhys Wilmot
2 Gary Neville	2 Darren Patterson ▮52
3 Denis Irwin	3 Dean Gordon
4 Steve Bruce	4 Gareth Southgate
5 Nicky Butt	5 Eric Young
6 Gary Pallister	6 Richard Shaw
7 Roy Keane ▮52	7 Ray Houghton
8 Paul Ince	8 Darren Pitcher
9 Ryan Giggs	(Ricky Newman)
(Brian McClair)	9 Chris Armstrong
10 Mark Hughes	10 Iain Dowie
11 Lee Sharpe	(Ian Cox)
	11 John Salako

For the real footy fans … here is the link for the above clip: https://youtu. be/y8bl8RwCha4

Conclusion: At the end of MARCH and during APRIL 1995, I frequently dreamt of football related incidents … which also included one of my nephews wearing his Manchester Utd football shirt! Perhaps this was to draw focus upon what was about to take place on the 7 APRIL? As I write about this now (3 JANUARY 2022) the dream has a perfect positive correlation with involvement of Man Utd fans.

I have located some online articles for this one. There is a white coach in the earlier picture and screen shots of news articles too. They mentioned the FA cup semi-final and its replay which also took place at Aston Villa's ground in Birmingham. It's no wonder they registered such a low crowd after all the violence surrounding the first match.

PS. After more hours trawling the internet, I found some additional information on a Crystal Palace fan forum. Apparently, an eyewitness stated that the Palace coach which pulled up outside the pub had men, women, and some children on it. As they were all getting off the vehicle, Man Utd supporters spilled out of the pub and furiously attacked them …which perfectly resembles my drawing. Paul Dixon was there and was stabbed while trying to protect some of their group. In the mayhem that followed, the coach driver tried to move out of the way but hadn't realised people were behind him … and ran over Paul's body. Simply awful. R.I.P … PD.

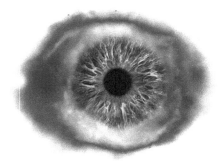

Oklahoma Office Bomb

Method: Lucid Dream—Tuesday 18 April 1995

Time before confirmation/evidence/proof: 2 days—TV and Newspaper articles.

Location/landmarks: A large, tall building.

People: Many Men/women/children.

Day or Night: Day (Sunny/dry).

Scene: Inside office corridors.

Colours: N/A

Smells: N/A

Vehicles: Not seen.

Feelings: Lack of urgency … no one is listening to me! I am shouting to everyone "Get out ... there's a bomb!

Dream Log: Precognition. Overview/copy of original log—after 4 previous dreams during the night I then found myself on a train carriage (in a toilet cubical) and was putting on a policeman's uniform … trousers, shirt, and jacket. Someone stood outside the train on a platform. I felt it was a policewoman, but I never saw anything other than a 'white' piece

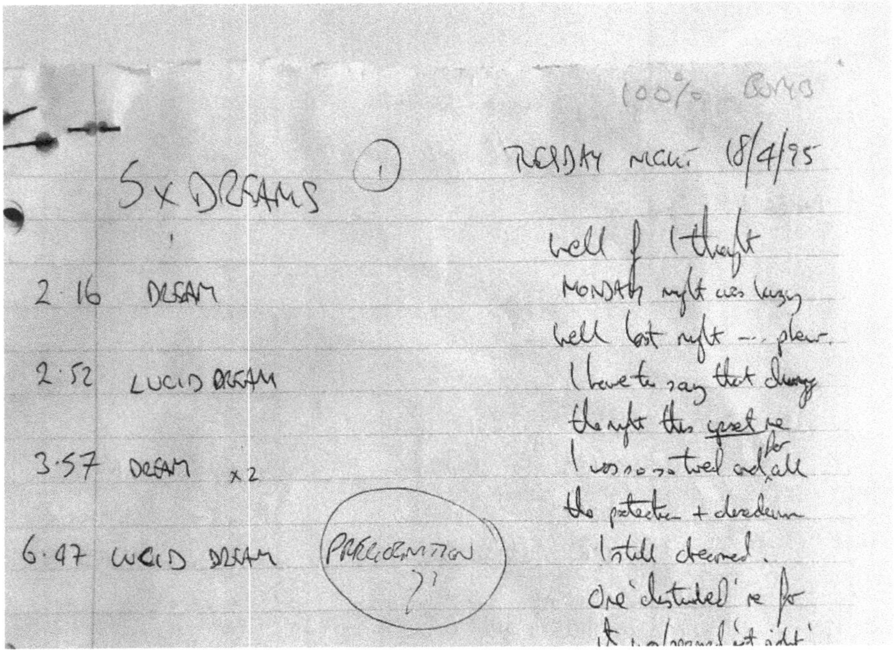
5 x DREAMS
TUESDAY NIGHT 18/4/95
2.16 DREAM
2.52 LUCID DREAM
3.57 DREAM x2
6.47 LUCID DREAM
PRECOGNITION
??

of material (a shirt?). It was as if being guarded. I turned around to reach for a hat. As I did so, I glimpsed 3 or 4 police (men?) out of the window walking from left to right. In my hand I had a beret … greyish, and it had an RAF (Royal Air Force) badge on it. I put it back on a hook, thinking that it wasn't right for me … for the uniform … or for this 'job'? Suddenly I had left the train and was running out of the station (everything blurred) and I heard some sort of alarm that went off.

I then found myself in a very large building … maybe a school or Tower block? Women and men were working in offices and there seemed to be lots of paperwork about. I ran about, "Get out now! There's a bomb! Everyone, evacuate the building … there's a bomb!" No one pays any attention. It is as if I'm not being heard! I go down another corridor and shout, "There's a bomb, everyone out." (Something about a package and get underneath a table?)

I think I have a radio in my hand, "Assistance, assistance … I need assistance!" STILL, no one is paying attention. Suddenly 3 women at a door are looking at me. (I'm standing at a doorway to another room). I say, "Get out now, there's a bomb!"

People have blank expressions on their faces. I'm looking at lady. She has curly hair. "Look do you have children?" I get no reply. "Just look at me ... what will it be like with just your head and no arms and legs? (It felt like I was implying how would they cope without her!)

I then have 'blurring' whereby my vision fades in and out. I am then in another corridor, and I see a pig, quite big and another further behind. I come across another door and a small boy carrying a piglet, He says, 'Can I take him with me?' "Of course," I said. I went into another room. Suddenly it's like looking into a farmyard, cattle, and sheep about everywhere ... almost like an auction ... but I only glimpse this 'scene'. Everything blurs over and I wake up at 6.47 am. Phew! I lay awake for a while after this. Was it a precognition? Normally something 'bad' usually is. We'll wait and see.

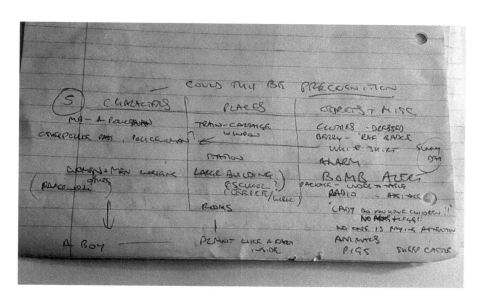

CUBICAL TOILET ??

TOILET CHANGED ?

I FOUND MYSELF ON A TRAIN CARRIAGE AND I WAS PUTTING ON A POLICEMAN'S 'UNIFORM', TROUSERS, SHIRT + JACKET. SOMEONE STOOD OUTSIDE THE TRAIN ON THE PLATFORM — I 'FELT' IT WAS A POLICEWOMAN BUT I NEVER SAW ANYTHING OTHER THAN A 'WHITE' PIECE OF MATERIAL (SHIRT ??) IT WAS

AS IF BEING A GUARDED

I TURNED AROUND TO REACH FOR A HAT. AS I DID SO, I GLIMPSED 3/4 POLICE (MEN?) (WATCHING FROM LEFT TO RIGHT) OUT OF THE WINDOW.

MY FAULT I USED TO BE IN THE RAF REGIMENT

IN MY HAND I HAD A BERET — GREYISH AND IT HAD AN R.A.F BADGE ON IT. I PUT IT BACK ON A HOOK THINKING THAT 'IT WASN'T RIGHT' (FOR ME? — FOR THE UNIFORM? FOR THIS JOB ??)

SUDDENLY I HAD LEFT THE TRAIN + WAS RUNNING OUT OF THE 'STATION' (EVERYTHING BLURRED) + I HEARD SOME SORT OF ALARM WENT OFF.

I THEN FOUND MYSELF IN A VERY LARGE BUILDING (MAYBE A SCHOOL? — TOWERBLOCK?

WOMEN + MEN WERE WORKING IN, LIKE OFFICES, AND THERE SEEMED TO BE LOTS OF PAPERWORK ABOUT.

I RAN ABOUT, 'GET OUT NOW' THERE'S A BOMB !! EVERYONE EVACUATE THE BUILDING — THERE'S A BOMB ! NO ONE PAYS ANY ATTENTION ITS AS IF I'M NOT BEING HEARD !

I GO DOWN ANOTHER CORRIDOR + SHOUT THERE'S A BOMB, EVERYONE OUT " ((SOMETHING ABOUT PACKAGE — GET — UNDER(NEATH) A TABLE ?? (I THINK ?)) I HAVE A RADIO IN MY HAND — " ASSISTANCE ASSISTANCE, I NEED ASSISTANCE ! "

STILL NO ONE IS PAYING ATTENTION SUDDENLY 3 WOMEN ARE AT A DOOR LOOKING AT ME.

CONT

I'M STANDING AT A DOORWAY TO ANOTHER ROOM

OFFICES

ME

2/3 women looked at me

CORE CORRIDOR

TYPE = WRITERS ON DESKS ETC

women

I SAY "GET AT NOW THREE A BOMB!"

PEOPLE HAVE BLANK EXPRESSION ON THEIR FACES
I LOOK AT A LADY. SHE HAS CURLY HAIR
"LOOK DO YOU HAVE CHILDREN!"
NO REPLY — JUST A LOOK AT ME
"WHAT WILL IT BE LIKE WITH JUST YOUR HEAD,
NO ARMS + LEGS!"

NB IT FELT LIKE I WAS IMAGINING "HOW WOULD THEY
COPE WITHOUT YOU!"

BLURRING

IN ANOTHER CORRIDOR
I SEE A PIG QUITE BIG AND ANOTHER
RUNNING BEHIND. I COME ACROSS ANOTHER DOOR
A SMALL BOY IS CARRYING A PIGLET. HE SAYS
CAN I TAKE HIM WITH ME. "OF COURSE" I SAID
I WENT INTO ANOTHER ROOM — I LOOK IN SUDDENLY
ITS LIKE LOOKING INTO A FARM YARD
CATTLE + SHEEP ABOUT EVERYWHERE ALMOST
LIKE AN AUCTION I ONLY GLIMPSE THIS
SCENE.

EVERYTHING BLURRS OVER
COAT + I WAKE UP PHEW!
6.47 AM.

I lay awake for a while after this. Was it
precognition ??
                    NORMALLY   SOMETHING BAD
USUALLY IS ?   will WAIT + SEE

SUNNY DAY
   TRAIN

Police conform.
POLICE
   STATION
WHITE/SHIRT

TALL BUILDING/SCHOOL?

   ROOMS
CORRIDORS
) OFFICES
TYPEWRITERS
PAPERWORK

RADIO

PIGS
ANIMALS

BOY

→

80

KILLED IN OFFICE BOMBING HORROR

From NEIL SYSON and CAROLINE GRAHAM in New York

MORE than 80 people were feared dead last night after a 1,200lb car bomb ripped *through* a U.S. government office block.

The victims included 17 young children — many of them playing in a second-floor creche.

They died instantly as the massive blast tore the front off the nine-storey building in Oklahoma City.

The bodies of 12 workers were found in one office on another floor, and scores more were feared buried beneath rubble in a collapsed underground car park.

A paramedic at the scene said: "We believe there are 75 bodies still inside."

The horror blast, heard 30 miles away, is thought to be the work of Arab terrorists.

Tinted

The FBI issued an alert for three "Middle Eastern" men seen driving away at speed after the explosion at the Alfred Murray Building.

The suspects were in a brown Chevrolet truck with tinted windows.

An FBI spokesman said: "Several unconfirmed reports are suggesting a Middle Eastern religious group may be involved."

In 1993, six died when New York's World Trade Centre was bombed by Muslim extremists.

The Arthur Murray Building houses 514 government staff. Six secret service agents were among the dead.

At least 100 injured victims were rushed to hospital. Sixty-five, including ten children, are critical.

'I thought the world had ended' — Pages 12, 13

KLAHOMA HORROR++OKLAHOMA HORROR++

Alive . . blood-spattered survivor sees a tot brought out

Agony . . . help for victim Gary Glover

SAVED

Brit mum tells how migraine stopped her being blown to bits in this

Rachel . . . 'Friends died instead of me'

Sun EXCLUSIVE

By CHRIS PHARO and NEIL SYSON

BRITON Rachel Mason escaped being blown apart in the Oklahoma bomb outrage — because of a headache.

Rachel, 27, who is training to be a U.S. policewoman, should have been on duty on the the ground floor of the wrecked building.

She would have had no chance of escape as the 1,200lb car bomb went off killing up to 200 people.

But instead she had taken the day off suffering from a migraine and was at home with her six-year-old daughter Caroline.

Divorcee Rachel, formerly a security guard in Swindon, Wilts, said yesterday: "I am in a state of shock, caught between relief and horror for all those who died. The most horrifying part of it is I could have taken Caroline to the creche that day where the oth children were killed." She went to "I'm heartbroken, many of the peop in that building had become frienc

"I still don't know whether any my colleagues were on duty in m place at the building when the bom went off. I'm praying I didn't se them to their death."

Harrowing

The massive blast at the Alfre Murrah office block shook Rachel home a 15-minute drive away.

She said "I switched on the TV an just couldn't believe my eyes. Th building where I should have bee was just a scene of blood, bodies an carnage."

Rachel is on a rota of volunteer helpers who should be taking part i the clean-up operation after th disaster.

But she admitted: "I'm terrified getting the call. I j don't know if I can cop with actually being o the scene – the TV pi tures were harrowin enough.

"I know I am ver lucky – but at the sam time I'm feeling a lot o pain and shock ove what has happened."

Her sister Claire, o Taunton, Somerset, sai Rachel is now havin second thoughts abou staying in America for police career.

Claire said: "It reall is an incredibly luck escape for her, but she deeply upset and shake by what has happene to her friends an colleagues.

Hopes of finding mor survivors were fadin last night.

Oklahoma mayor Ro Norick revealed tha there were 900 people i

LAST ONE OUT ALIVE

RESCUE doctor Rick Nelson told last night how he pulled out the last survivor — a 15-year-old girl called Brandy.

He said: "I was outside the building waiting to bring out the dead bodies when the firemen heard a voice.

"She was under a mass of concrete, twisted metal and conduit beams.

"We basically had to dig very very gingerly to prevent things from falling on her or us and very carefully cut beams and conduits."

Dr Nelson went on: "Sometimes she com- plained of difficulty in breathing. That was very scary.

"We could not see her. We could see just the tip of her foot and I was lying on a dead body.

"When we got her away we felt more comfortable. The greatest thing was when she told us she loved us."

Brandy is "critical but stable" in hospital.

KLAHOMA HORROR++OKLAHOMA HORROR++

BY MY HEADACHE

AS IT WAS

Soft target . . the Federal Government building

AS IT IS

...rnae . . the office block 'looked like it was put in a blender' after the massive Oklahoma bomb blast

...uilds when the exploded — far than the original ...stes around 500. ...ter ...gs continued ...ack through the ...e . . . signs of life. ...56-strong urban and rescue team Arizona was work-with fibre optic ...al acoustic as ...al devices in the ...of denoting some-...reath...

Cries

...kers who bought ...arge steel girder to ...up the middle of ...uilding ...ughout the night ...and ...our giant ...ights ...pped the ...nteer Mi-...Dyke said: ...was ...erywhere

Every building you walked by, there was blood on it. There was a man split in half. All we could do was cover him up."

Paramedic John Griffith said: "It's like they took an office and put it in a blender."

Rescue doctor Gary Massad told how one survivor, 28-year-old Amy Petty, had to have a leg sawn off without anaesthetic to get her out from under a concrete beam.

He said: "She didn't have anything but her willpower to fight the pain."

Amy said afterwards from her hospital bed: "A guy held my hand. They were really wonderful, but it was very scary. It was very painful, but I knew they had

to do it." Terry Jones, a medical technician, said: "I just took part in a surgery where a little boy had part of his brain hanging out.

"You tell me, how can anyone have so little respect for human life?"

Chaplain George Young said: "The bulk of the babies are still inside. We're bracing for the worst."

TOT PULLED FROM RUBBLE IS DEAD

A baby whose picture was shown around the world as a symbol of the carnage has died from its injuries.

The un-named tot was carried out by fireman Chris Fields who said: "This makes me want to throw up."

TORIES' TERROR JIBE AT CLINTON

By PASCOE WATSON

TORY MPs last night tore into Bill Clinton in the wake of the Oklahoma bomb over his support for Sinn Fein leader Gerry Adams.

Andrew Hunter, chairman of the backbench Northern Ireland Committee, said: "We sympathise deeply with the people of Oklahoma.

"But we ask President Clinton: Does he now understand the dangers of befriending IRA supporters and apologists like Gerry

Adams?" Fellow Tory David Wilshire wrote to U.S. ambassador Admiral William Crowe.

He said: "I would be fascinated to learn how he is able to differentiate between these terrorists and the foreign-funded IRA killers."

...orld today

Bringing you the latest national and
international news, from the
UK News press agency and Reuters

...igest

**...ury at
...r politics'**

...MPs have reacted
to a Labour Party
which branded Prime
...ohn Major a liar.
...ervices Minister David
last night's broadcast,
...he run-up to the May 4
...ctions, saw Labour
...to "gutter politics".

...es to PC

...for a man wanted in
...n with the murder of
...p Walters continued
...olleagues paid tribute
...year-old probationary

...men were being
...about the shooting in
...t London, after being
...ar the scene.

...ut down

...ught as a birthday gift
...year-old boy had to be
...after it was chased,
...tortured by teenagers
...ill, West Midlands.
...nspector Tim Scott
...the attack as
...bly cruel, callous and

...gas doubt

...authorities have
...are not sure what
...gas was used in the
...okohama's railway
...erday.

...an 400 people were
...what police fear was a
...e Tokyo subway gas
...h killed 12 people and
...ausands last month.

...ven cannabis

...re today seeking a
...aths who gave a five-
...oy cannabis as he
...r his home. Trevor
...gered home and sat
...n the sofa after
...old him to smoke a
...nt.

...ent happened on the
...ate in Peterborough,
...parents took him to
...here urine samples
...he had breathed in
...n.

...loss

...ES girl cost her
...£111,000 after
...to buy their
...National Lottery
...chelle Ulukus'
...Birmingham were
...a lottery windfall
...ld them she had
...uy their ticket.
...member Joanne
...said: "We felt like
...out of the window.
...regular numbers
...plus the bonus

...howdown

...health workers
...itain were set for a
...today.Hundreds of
...were converging on
...al to lobby
...s as anger at the
...one per cent pay
...aff mounted.

■ **AFTERMATH . . . an aerial shot showing the extent of the blast damage**

Deaths mount in terror blast

■ **RESCUE . . . firefighters bring out one of the survivors**

AT LEAST 31 people were confirmed dead today after a massive car bomb tore apart a US government building in Oklahoma City.

More than 300 people were still missing after the worst terrorist outrage in American history.

Rescue workers were continuing their grim search for bodies thought to be trapped under the collapsed floors of the devastated Alfred Murrah building.

Oklahoma Assistant Fire Chief Jon Hansen said at least 31 people had died in the bombing, including twelve children.

But he warned the death toll was expected to rise.

At least 200 injured people, most suffering from cuts, scrapes and a broken bones, were treated in hospitals as the city declared itself a disaster zone.

As the hunt began for those responsible, the finger of blame pointed at either Islamic extremists or fanatics seeking revenge for the FBI raid which ended the Waco siege two years to the day ago.

Mr Hansen said rescuers were having problems getting through the rubble to bodies trapped under collapsed floors of the nine-storey building.

A 15-year-old girl was pulled out alive from the wreckage last night and was rushed to hospital in a critical condition.

Two people who were also rescued yesterday later died from their injuries.

Mr Hansen said the number of rescue workers searching through the wreckage had been limited to 40 because of fears that the whole building might collapse.

Bomb like a quake says survivor

DAZED survivors of the huge explosion in Oklahoma told of their horror and narrow escape from the devastated office block.

Wandering the streets, many could barely describe what had happened to them because they were so badly shocked.

Fleets of ambulances and paramedics were on hand to treat and comfort survivors.

Scores wandered aimlessly hardly able to believe the enormity of the blast which ripped an entire wall from the nine-storey Alfred Murrah building.

One US Department of Agriculture worker said: "...thought it was an earthquake — dived under my desk and the glass all fell in. It was almost slow motion."

A colleague said: "Whoever d...

ON THE

*It was like a dream,
just not real*
— US Department of
Agriculture worker
pulled from the
Oklahoma City wreckage

RECORD

this and what could be the motive?"

Brian Espy, who was working on the fifth floor of the building said: "Thank God, I'm alive."

He added: "I was working on project when the explosion occurred. My entire staff of seven people is gone."

The massive car bomb ripped through the building without warning in a city which had never felt the shadow of war terrorist atrocities.

The blast – which sent slivers glass flying over six blocks acted like a giant can opener peeling away one wall.

Officials said the bomb destroyed more than half of nine-storey building, gutting several floors.

Office workers, many of them bleeding, staggered in shock into the streets.

Injured victims lay bleeding on the sidewalk.Miraculously, two babies, a boy and a girl both under 12 months old, escaped unscathed.

The marble and concrete facade of the building tumbled into the streets, crushing vehicles...

On This Day

April 20 Thurs

● 1912 Irish writer Bram Stoker, noted for his classic novel Dracula, died in London.
● 1913 Dancer Isadora Duncan's two children, Deidre (7) and Patrick (5) drowned when their car crashed into the Seine in France.
● 1968 122 people were killed when a Boeing 707 bound for London crashed in South Africa.
● 1969 British troops were called into Northern Ireland to guard key installations after nine Belfast post

● Leslie Phillips, actor, pictured, 71
● Johnny Tillotson, American country and pop singer, 56
● Ryan O'Neal, actor, pictured, 54
● Ray Brooks, actor, 56

offices were fire-bombed, a bus station attacked and the city's main reservoir damaged.
● 1974 A Catholic man was shot in Belfast to became the 1,000th victim of

the unrest in Northern Ireland.
...see Long-distance lorry driver Ashwell was arrested in Greece customs officials discovered part Iraqi supergun loaded on his truck

12 bodies lay in my office..like the world had ended

Fleeing the carnage ... frightened people rush away in panic from the wrecked building after hearing a second bomb had been discovered

By CAROLINE GRAHAM

A WEEPING woman pulled from the devastation of one of America's worst terrorist outrages yesterday said: "There were 12 bodies in my office — it was like the end of the world."

...and a man who escaped with his life said: "It just went boom. There were bodies covered in blood everywhere."

About 500 people were working in the Alfred Murray Federal building in Oklahoma City when it was rocked by the blast.

As rescuers searched for those feared trapped under rubble, State Governor Frank Keating said: "There has been a considerable loss of life."

...the pictures no can't put a figure on it but it has to be multiple and very bad."

The Governor was expected to declare the site an emergency area.

The massive car bomb explosion blew away an entire wall of the nine-storey building. It blew out windows for two blocks around and hundreds of people on their way to work were hit by flying glass. Others already in their offices staggered into the streets in shock.

Cars were set on fire and a plume of black smoke spread over the city of 450,000 people.

The blast ruptured gas mains and police appealed for people to evacuate the area. Authorities also evacuated nearby 50 Penn Plaza where the FBI has its local office.

FBI spokesman Dan Vogel said: "We have to consider this as a crime scene. Obviously it's a very big crime scene. We are not ruling out anything at this point."

The city's St Anthony's Hospital called in all its off-duty staff and the Red Cross sent out an SOS for blood donors as the injured were rushed in by ambulances and private cars.

Hospital staff were unable to locate the parents of two tiny babies — a boy and girl under 11 months old.

...who were discovered, amazingly unharmed in the rubble.

One survivor fell more than 50ft from the fifth floor before landing in the rubble of the damaged block.

He told rescuers: "It was like just falling. I felt down through the air. I didn't know what was happening."

He was treated for multiple injuries including a broken leg, ankle and stomach ribs.

Another survivor said: "There was this huge bang.

"It was like nine metres. I dived under the desk and then the glass came down and the ceiling caved in. When I came out I could see the sky through a hole in the roof. There just wasn't any building left."

And another told: "It looks just like Beirut."

An elderly man who escaped down a fireman's ladder from the fifth floor said: "There were three of us and we were just knocked on our backs. I managed to get under a desk just as the ceiling came down. That saved me."

A woman said: "We had to crawl on our stomachs and feel our way out. There was thick smoke and glass everywhere.

Trapped

"Not everyone got out. I could hear people screaming they were trapped."

The building houses government offices, including an army recruitment centre which was worst hit.

David Martin, a national security officer said: "There seems to have been a great deal of destruction in that one small office. There were many injuries and one civilian is missing."

"There was a man in the office who had one child killed and one injured."

In Washington, the White House said President Bill Clinton was "very troubled" by news of the explosion. Spokesman Mike McCurry and Attorney General Janet Reno had dispatched an FBI team to the site and that White House chief of staff Leon Panetta was to convene a meeting to prepare a further federal response.

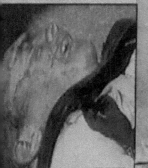

...an injured man cries as blood pours from his wounds

Alive!...a fireman carries out a tiny, battered survivor

SIMILARITY'S

① Tall building felt like school ✓

② Bomb office workers paperwork everywhere

③ Ref to children no arms + legs

④ Corridors/hallways sunny weather

or could relate to American military??

DIFFERENCES

① My uniform black (shirt white?)

① USA police - different belt comm what they blue shirt)

② why 5G alerted in the building almost like attack?

③ why 5G bare?

Remove a badge before leaving - now suggests in Ireland (or abroad)

④'s army - not - on confirmation scale

conclusion

I have split way given me association on an inclusive scale

BOMB BLAST: 300 MISSING

RESCUE WORKERS say they c
still hear cries of help fro
people trapped under the rubb
from a huge car bomb bla
which tore apart a governme
building in Oklahoma City.

Thirty-one bodies have been taken o
of the devastated building and mo
than 300 people are still missing afte
yesterday's blast. The dead include
children.

At least 200 injured people, most suffering fro
cuts, scrapes and a broken bones, were treated
hospitals as the city declared itself a disast
zone.

As the hunt began for those responsible, th
finger of blame pointed at Islamic extremists
fanatics seeking revenge for the FBI raid whic
ended the Waco siege two years to the day ago.

Oklahoma assistant fire chief Jon Hansen sa
rescuers were having problems getting throug
the rubble to bodies trapped under collapse
floors of the nine-storey building.

He said:"There's a lot of bodies in there."

● **Full report and more pictures – page 4**

■ **ABOVE** : the Oklahoma county sheriff brings out a baby
injured in the blast
■ **RIGHT** : the federal building, reduced to a wreck

Hot shots!   **Picture special on the ET's
Penalty Shootout '95 – page 47**

Conclusion: The evidence from television and newspapers reports provides a strong positive correlation. The interesting aspect of this— until my mind/consciousness/visual blurred over and I met the little boy—was that absolutely no one was paying any attention to my presence or reasoning. Like I was a 'ghost'. On the face of things, this felt like I knew what was going to happen, but I could not prevent it from occurring. Perhaps I helped in some small way, but 'fate' still has to be played out?

The first part of the dream at the train station could be a destination between dimensions and realms of reality. The police uniform is symbolic. Police can represent angels or divine protection. It's like I was there to help, but this is not my permanent job/role, hence the beret. 'If the cap fits wear it' is a popular expression … but I was also in the RAF for a while in my younger days. Perhaps I was there in some small capacity, perhaps even if it was to help that little boy.

It's strange how my presence came across the animals. It might have been a separate dream entirely, but there were children there in the America Kids Day care centre on the building's second floor. Could the centre have had toys, stuffed animals, and the like? The building also had agricultural workers, though, but that could be a loose connection entirely!

The very tall building reference is accurate. There were some 500 people in the Alfred Murray Federal building in Oklahoma City. The offices/corridors/paperwork connections all match. And, if you can read the newspaper reports, it sites one man managed got under a desk just a ceiling came down. I mention a package in the original log, but the cause was a bomb placed in a truck. They killed 168 people, including 19 children. More than 500 were injured … as the explosion also affected nearly 300 buildings.

The authorities first suspected Middle Eastern terrorist groups, but 2 men, Timothy McVeigh, and Terry Nichols (both formerly U.S. Army Rangers and anti-government extremists) were later convicted. McVeigh became the first person executed for a federal crime in the U.S since 1963 and Nichols avoided the death penalty and was sentenced to life in prison.

Ford Capri Car Crash

Method: Lucid Dream—Monday 8 May 1995.

Time before confirmation/evidence/proof: 11 days—TV and Newspaper articles.

Location/landmarks: Main Road, car speeding along.

People: Not seen.

Day or Night: Evening/night.

Scene: A car speeding … then somersaulting towards me.

Colours: Red (danger/death).

Smells: N/A

Vehicles: Car (Ford Capri).

Feelings: Viewing a car completely out of control. Voice/ energy/spirit guide with me asking me to clarify the colour.

Dream Log: Precognition, vision/dream. Suddenly it's like I am watching a scene on a giant TV. A car (red), is crashing, somersaulting straight towards me (my vision). Over and over, it goes on its nose/side/bonnet end to end. It goes down a road for ages—maybe off a roundabout. Suddenly it's like I'm looking down from a great height, like over a motorway and I say, "Oh, that's that red car!" A voice says, 'Are you sure?' (As if 'someone' is with me) ... "Yes, it looks like a CAPRI". Everything faded and I woke up ... frantically scribbling notes with my pen.

As I looked down, the car looked like this (see original drawings below), more like a sports car really—yet I said, 'CAPRI' ... as if I was sure of myself. NB. I would have known the difference because it has always been my favourite car!

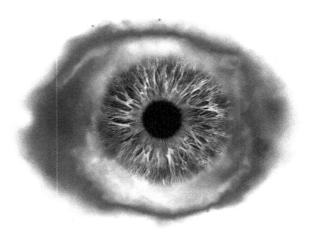

CHARACTERS	PLACES	OBJECTS + MISC
③ Me (+ screen the + voice)	On ground IN AIR	— LIKE WATCHING A TV SCREEN / FILM
		CAR ACCIDENT — (CAUSE + EFFECT)
PRECOGNITION ??		RED CAR ? — SPORTS — (CAPRI ??)

PRECOGNITION

DESCRIPTION

Suddenly its like I'm watching a scene on a giant TV.

A car, red is crashing, somersaulting straight towards me (my vision). over + over it goes on its (nose / side) end to end. It goes down (barrel)

a road for ages — maybe off a roundabout.

roundabout ??

↓ Falling went over

vision Blurred over it

Suddenly its like I'm looking down from a great height — like over a Motorway. And I say "oh there's that red car!" A voice says "Are you sure?" (As I screech with me). "Yes it looks like a CAPRI" Everything faded and I woke up

(PTO)

(CONT

As I looked down — the car looked like this - more like a .
Sports car really — yet it had CAPRI - and sure of myself.

CARS GOING BY

ROAD

AS IF CAR ZOOMED

Could this be after the roof has been ripped off??
After accident??

100%
SPIRITUAL
PRECOGNITIVE

19/5/55
CONFIRMED
PRECOGNITIVE

CRASH HAPPENED
NEAR M 1 Motorway
Actual
Scene
CORN Fields
car off
road ? here
ACCIDENT
FAULT OCCURED   18/5/
(CAUSE + EFFECT)

THE
ACTUALLY VIEWED
NEWS BROADCAST
OF THE REPORT OF
THIS PRECOGNITION

NB CAR WAS BLACK
NOT RED. MY PRECOGN
RED = DANGER
= DEATH.

MEANINGS:- Red =   Lowest rate of vibration.
Precognition - or come back down to earth with a bump. (??)

Flying.   =   Ability to use higher realms of consciousness
Expansion.

VOICE:-   Voice of the teacher (my guide last night)

To dream of an accident is a warning to avoid any
mode of travel for a short period as you are threatened with loss of
life

(WOOW—   OUR CAR IS A PURPLEY RED CAPRI !!
I'll need to watch out / drive very carefully

ANALYSIS }
CONCLUSION }   ___   / yet that doesn't feel right

/ I feel its precognitive yet I saw
newspaper (?EST)

+ I WAS RIGHT!

Wreck . . . Sally London's crumpled Capri after cops turned it back over

RIDDLE OF CAR SMASH BODY COPS DIDN'T SPOT

By JAMIE PYATT

A WOMAN was found dead in her overturned car yesterday 24 hours after cops examined the wreck and reported no sign of her.

Two officers saw the mangled Ford Capri in a field on Wednesday morning and slapped on a 'Police Aware' sticker.

The 34-year-old's body was only discovered yesterday when a roadsweeper spotted her arm sticking from a window.

Last night a post mortem was being held to discover how Sally London died and if she was still ALIVE in the wreck when police first checked it.

A police source said: "We don't know if she died instantly or was alive with terrible injuries.

"But in the 24 hours she was there she could have bled to death."

Her husband Les was stunned that papa could miss her body.

Check

He said at his home in Lidlington, Beds, last night: "How on earth did the police not see her? It seems they didn't check the car.

"I just want her back. But I know I can't have her."

Les, 49, was separated from Mrs London, but said they were still close.

He reported her missing on Tuesday evening when she failed to show up at his house.

Film worker Les spent Wednesday looking for her — and arrived home to find a scribbled note from police, asking him to collect his wife's car.

Victim Sally is found next day

He sobbed last night: "I phoned the police and I said 'My wife is missing — have you checked if she is in the car?'

"They arranged that my son James would meet them where the car was."

James, 17, drove to the scene to find police with the body.

Les, who has two teenage children by another marriage, said: "I still love my wife dearly.

"Sally moved out because basically she wasn't getting on with my son James, but we still kept in touch."

The crash happened at a well-known accident blackspot in Ridgmont, Beds. Farmer Alan Fuller said: "I am always pulling wrecks out of the field with my tractor."

Mrs London, a solicitor's receptionist, used to help at church fairs in Lidlington.

Vicar John Greenway said: "The whole village will be shocked."

MURDER CLUE

UM of three battered to death at her farmhouse may kept a mystery apment the night she

new witness says she anet Brown, 51, at heel of her Volvo was revealed on

TV's Crimewatch last night when husband Graham, 53, announced a £10,000 reward.

Janet was found naked and handcuffed at £340,000 Hall Farm at Radnage, Bucks, on April 11. Police believe the disturbed a burglar.

---

4   EVENING TELEGRAPH, Friday, May 19, 1995

World tod

NEWS Digest

Ebola fears

A WOMAN and her two children were today in an isolation unit in London following fears they had contracted the deadly Ebola virus.

They flew into Britain from Zaire via Moscow and fell ill yesterday while visiting a Home Office immigration centre in Croydon, south-west London.

Crash blunder

POLICE pushed a note through a man's door asking him to collect his wife's wrecked car — not knowing she had died in the crash.

Officers stuck a "Police Aware" sticker on the wreckage of the car in Bedfordshire unaware 40-year-old Sally-Ann London was inside. Her body was found 24-hours later by a council roadsweeper.

ON THE

Conclusion: The TV and newspaper confirmation appeared 11 days later. The driver, Sally London, unfortunately died in the accident. It is very sad to read that she was found dead, 24 hours after the police examined the wreck and placed the usual 'police aware' notice on the vehicle. Could she have survived if she had been spotted?

Time and time again, I'm viewing such tragedies. This occasion was like watching a TV ... and the scene as if it's about to play out in front of me. I believe this case has strong correlation with the make of car, the main road and what I thought was a cornfield (in part two of my original log and the side image I drew). I realize the colour of the car (which I saw as red but was in fact black) can be called into question, but I think this obviously signified danger/death.

And the voice asking me whether I was sure the car was red is quite unusual in my precognitive experiences ... almost like it was my soul, or a spirit guide or God teaching me, checking my abilities, or guiding me to become clearer at what I am observing or doing within the dream/vision. But why can't I identify the exact names or precise locations? Could I–or will I–ever be able to help prevent such things? Or perhaps this just isn't my purpose or goal. Once again, the age-old question of our fate and destiny and karma fills my mind and heart. RIP Sally London.

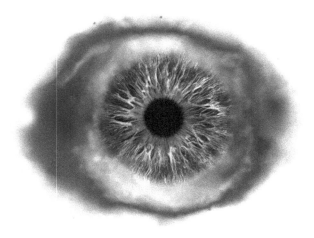

Vaal Reefs Mining Accident

Method: Lucid Dream—Monday 8 May 1995.

Time before confirmation/evidence/proof: 4 days—TV and Newspaper articles.

Location/landmarks: Cave/Mine.

People: Group of men.

Day or Night: Blackness.

Scene: Me/group of men.

Colours: Yellow/gold.

Smells: N/A

Vehicles: N/A

Feelings: It was like I was seeing men in a cave ... bright yellow/gold light above. Almost like before something was to happen. And yet a feeling of me trying to rescue them. Sense of being watched.

Dream Log: This might sound weird, but sometimes we (as souls) do 'spiritual' rescue work, whereby we visit people/places/different dimensions to help others. This can also involve helping within the animal kingdom too.

In one of 3 dreams tonight, I sensed a tragic event, but also felt I had the privilege of helping rescue and direct soul's 'home'. Some of the imagery in my original dream log (further below) seemingly depict some sort of basic rescue apparatus but may also symbolize the connection to what happened ... with winches being 'broken'?

I found myself 'watching' at first, and then in the dream itself. Someone had either trapped (on purpose?) or a number of people in a well, or a cave/mine. It was as if someone near me just watched and wasn't able to (or didn't want to) help ... either the people or me. WAS IT A TEST? Somehow, I managed to get the rope/winch working using a 'bar' of some sort, and it was by pumping my arms upwards that the winch or rope could move up. (It was a real struggle).

One by one the people came up and once the last one was up the man turned around and said, 'You're a good bloke you are', or something to this effect, 'Bloody good bloke' (possibly.) I smiled and then everything faded with the feeling that I was being watched.

I feel this was a spiritual test. Could I ... would I help others. I think I did okay ... I hope so anyway!

These are my original dream notes below. Once again, please forgive my handwriting, I did go to school once! The thing is, when you're half asleep and trying to get as much information down as quickly as possible, punctuation and legibility goes out of the window!

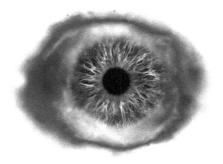

DREAMS (X)   (P. 3)   TUES
FLASHES (X)   LUCID   9TH / 5 / 1995

CHARACTERS	PLACES	OBJECTS + MISC
Me	CAVE + MINE	A test ??
Gang of men		winch — well/hole
+ Caroline ??		rope — BAR
A guide.		A Rescue ??

③

+ felt
+ at one point
Caroline was there
but I couldn't be sure

DESCRIPTION   I found myself 'watching' at first and then
in the dream itself.

Someone had either trapped (on purpose?) or a
~~it was not working~~ number of people in a well, or a cave/mine
Either that or some sort of winch had been broken.
It was as if someone nearby just watched or wasn't
able to (or did not wish to) help ... either the people or me.
(OR WAS IT A TEST! (?))   I had to help those people I knew it

Somehow I managed to get
the rope, winch working using a 'bar' of some sort and it was
by pumping my arms upwards that the winch, or rope could move
up. (IT WAS A REAL STRUGGLE)
One by one the people came up and once the last one was up
— the men, turned around and said "Your a good bloke you are"
(or something to this effect 'Bloody good bloke" (possibly)   I smiled and
then everything faded with the feeling that I was being watched

CONT

Some sort of light
Yellow Glow

Inside cave / well?

It was as if I could see them inside for a split record?

Some part of the pulley broke + on floor / stand

ROPE

BAR??
up + down

Me pulling a rope, but lifting each person up one at a time.

'Someone else watching

Rescue? — To rescue others, foretells that you will be esteemed for your good deeds.

MEANINGS: well, cave, mine)
ROPE

— To be in a cave foreshadows change.
You will probably be estranged from those who are very dear from you

Cord connecting us to the physical bodies, or an emotional connection to others. If tied to / by rope it is limitation, if breaking free — expansion

well: - To see a well a pump in it shows you will have opportunities to advance your prospects

ANALYSIS }
CONCLUSION }

I feel — a Spiritual test — could I, would I? help others.

(I feel I did okay 1 h
so anyway!

in arctic

100 miners killed as lift falls 1,400ft

elegir

MORE than 100 gold miners were feared dead last night after a lift plunged nearly 1,400ft.

It's cable snapped when a pit train jumped rails, and crashed down the lift shaft.

The impact reduced the lift to half its size. President Nelson Mandela was "shocked" by the horror at the mine near Orkney, South Africa.

HOME MOVIES

Film-crazy Alan Short, 63, has built a nine-seat cinema in the garden of his Bristol home.

WED EVENT
10TH MAY 95

His close friend Donald Polson today said he believed the burglars knew Mr Paliunovas, 73, struck the bonanza in January.

But he said the multi-millionaire pensioner kept only small sums of cash at his Gloucester home.

ON THE

> Privatisation is no more responsible for those job losses that it is for an outbreak of measles
> – Prime Minister John Major countering claims that rail privatisation caused the closure of ABB Transportation in York

RECORD

Dog reward

TOP racehorse trainer Guy Harwood has offered a £500 reward for the return of his favourite gun dog, Bella.

The labrador ran off two weeks

Mine gives up its dead

WORKERS wait near the top of a mineshaft for rescuers to bring to the surface the bodies of miners killed in this South African gold mine.

More than 100 workers are believed to have been killed after an underground train plunged down a shaft onto a lift.

Rescue teams have so far recovered 47 bodies.

Vaal Reefs is a gold bearing reef which is mined near the town of Orkney in <u>Dr Kenneth Kaunda District Municipality</u> in the <u>North West</u> province of <u>South Africa</u>. The town of Orkney is home to a large gold mining operation originally owned by <u>AngloGold Ashanti</u>, a company that was originally incorporated in 1944 under the name of Vaal Reefs Exploration and Mining Company Limited. (Source Wikipedia). On the 10 MAY 1995, 105 men perished at the Anglo-American Corporation's Vaal Reefs Mine near Orkney, southwest of Johannesburg. Even a nation hardened to mining tragedy was horrified by the gruesome disaster at one of South Africa's largest and most profitable gold mines. Miners had finished their shift in the sweltering depths of the 2.3 km (1.4 mi) Shaft Number Two and were returning to the surface in an elevator cage. High above, their fate was sealed when an underground train entered a tunnel that was supposed to be closed, went out of control, and careered into the shaft at the edge of 56 level (1,676 m below surface). The falling train hit elevator cables, sending the cage plunging downwards in free fall … 1,500 feet (460 m). A second after it hit bottom (2,300 m below surface), the heavy locomotive smashed into the already compressed cage and further reduced the substantial two-tier structure to what the President of South Africa's National Union of Mineworkers (NUM) later described as 'a one-floor tin box'. The occupants were pulverized, body parts were scattered everywhere and identifying individuals proved to be a long and distressing process. Two days after the accident a representative of Anglo-American grimly told a press conference: 'The bodies are badly mutilated, it's hot and they're beginning to decompose'. The NUM established a trust fund for dependents of victims, who were located as far apart as the rural areas of Lesotho, Transkei, Swaziland, and Botswana.

NB. The one person who did actually survive the catastrophic accident was the driver of the runaway train, who managed to jump clear before it toppled into Shaft Number Two and fell towards the rapidly ascending elevator cage.

Conclusion: In terms of my original drawings inside the cave/mine could have been before the miners got into the elevator and their fateful trip to the surface.

There was the yellow/gold light, which I believe indicated the gold mine we were in. One could also say it was the light of God shining over them all.

The reference to winches could have been related with the elevator cords and cables, but also any manner of equipment being used in the attempt to rescue those below. Had I just been an observer to this tragedy or involved in the spiritual rescue as a guide for these souls? As I hadn't seen the large building shaft above ground and initially no inkling of the country (though that seems obvious now), but with a strong correlation worthy of a precognition case.

Thank heavens the miners involved would have passed away quickly ... and I'm so pleased that their families/ dependents were eventually given financial support.

Here is the memorial of the disaster in Johannesburg, South Africa in which the miners lost their lives. Since then, the government there has committed to improving safety conditions underground. This tragedy brought two key changes to the mining industry. Firstly, the immediate implementation of the new Health & Safety Act—specifically the five basic rights—and secondly, for the first time ever, the stakeholders took care of the dependants after the death of breadwinners.

PRECOGNITION 11

RAF Tornados Collision

Method: Dream 2—Thursday 5 October 1995.

Time before confirmation/evidence/proof: 25 days—TV (30 October 1995) and Newspaper articles (31 October 1995).

Location/landmarks: Runway and mid-air.

People: Not seen clearly.

Day or Night: Night.

Scene: Me watching 2 military aircraft take off ... then something shoots upward / ejected, a brilliant light overhead.

Colours: Red and blue and 'colours' plus white light.

Smells: N/A

Vehicles: Aircraft x 2, helicopter.

Feelings: Something shoots upwards ... hits the aircraft?

Dream Log: Before I went to bed, I gazed upon the moon for 5 mins ... only 3 days until its full. I prayed for love and light and thought of White Cloud, a 'spirit' guide. Incredible sensations were running through me, and images too. Indian faces and a teepee, a face to the left and a teepee like this, someone just inside it (See original dream log further below). Wonderful! Thank you all.

I awoke at 3.14 a.m. yet had no recall whatsoever (sorry) then fell back asleep. Then, I received two further dreams, waking up at 6.14 a.m. about 10 seconds before my alarm clock (thanks for the sleep spirit). I frantically scramble for my pen and paper as surely the second one was a precognition!

OVERVIEW: Me—watching ... a runway. 2 x planes/military aircraft. Such power, elegance, manoeuvers. 2 x Tornados. So, so silent. (No sound at all heard). Light/flare or anti-air missile? A light ... looking at planes. First thought ... helicopter, in distance. but is it like 'the light of man'? My first thoughts (inside the dream) were they symbolism ... Tornados (WINDS) so silent, but deadly?

FIRST THOUGHTS (dream description from notes): Then, as if there were two dreams connected (or continued) ... it starts just as many times before, as if I'm in the air 'looking' (or watching a TV screen). Suddenly in the distance I see what resembles a runway, its nighttime.

Suddenly a white dot, flash comes up and darts away. I then see two aircraft—military—everything is uncannily silent. I see the red, blue and coloured afterburn as they go high in the air (split second) from their engines. The white dot comes back up from the ground as I look and think an aircraft missile or anti-aircraft missile deflected/ejected from the aircraft. (Dot going down or up?)

They bank to the right, and I see fully loaded undercarriages then 'out of the blue', a searing white light comes from nowhere as if to light them up ... to show more of them to me. I say to myself – they are Tornados. The white light resembles a helicopter search light, but I then say to myself—it can't be—how can a helicopter be at the same level or speed as a plane?

Everything fades to a distance, and then as if I get no pause, I go straight to another scene (dream three). When I woke up, I was thinking two things, A) I was 99% sure that the aircraft represent 2 x TORNADOS—AS THEY ARE AN ENGLISH AIRCRAFT OR B) SYMBOLISM—2 x DEVASTING BITS OF WEATHER TO HIT UK. (Using the amount of bombs/weapon load to indicate the force of them and it will happen at night. Nb. Tornados/aircraft were also used in war e.g., Bosnia Sarajevo.

PRECOGNITION? ✓ ① (YES) 100%
MILITARY
AIRCRAFT 5/10/95

3 x DREAMS   TWO   NIGHT
   2 CONNECTED

③ 3 days to a full moon. I gazed upon it
for about 5 mins / prayed for love + light. Thought
of W. Cloud etc. Incredible sensations running
through me, + images too. Indian faces + a
teepee ('a face to the right _ a face to the left and
teepee like this
wonderful! Thankyou all, ② Someone just inside it

① — 3·14 AM ⟨auuck⟩
   recall ??

no
recall
sorry

① Space :-
DREAM 1   NO RECALL !!

12 PRECOGNITION

TORNADO ✓
AIRCRAFT

* 25 DAYS BEFORE X
   EVENT !!

Cont. X

DREAM 2

DREAMS
→ ②
↓ +
③
Separated by
2 pauses?

Awoke
6.14 AM
about 10 secs
before alarm

Thanks guys
for the sleep
last night!

Me + watching.   (in air)

2 x PLANES / AIRCRAFT   MILITARY,
                         AIRCRAFT
                                    SUCH POWER   MANOEUVRES ELEGANCE

A LIGHT - LOOKING AT PLANES

DOG   DREAM 3
        ON TOP - UP OF
AT A OLD CASTLE / CHURCH. BUILDING
(SOME SORT OF   SHIP / AIRSHIP
(PEOPLE   IN IT, WINDOWS.

DOG   MASTIFF VICIOUS.
        AS IF WAITING FOR ME - TO GET ME? }

THROUGH A VILLAGE.?
CUDDLEY TOY

light / flare
(in the air - moon?
                         2 x   TORNADO
                              (SO DO SILENT
First thought helecopter but =
light of moon? IN DISTANCE

moonlight.

WAVING AT

LOOK DOWN
STONE STEP
COMES TO ME
FIRST FEAR - (
GIVE IT LOVE + A
BANNANA (??)
I WALK AWAY.
THINKING - DOG
GETS IT.   AS
IF NOW A FRIEND + I P
IT, PLAY WITH TOY IN TH

PAUSE   NEXT DREAM 2 ↓
          (FIRST THOUGHTS   - TORNADOES / WINDS - SO SILENT BUT AR

NOT RELATED
TO
DREAM ③

Just as many times before - as if I'm in the air looking or
watching a TV screen.   Suddenly in the distance I see
what resembles a runway   - its night time. Suddenly a
white dot, flash comes up and darts away. I then see
two aircraft - military -   everything is uncannily silent
I see the red, blue + coloured afterburn as they go high
into the air (split second) from their engines. The white
dot comes back as if up from the ground as I look + think
aircraft missile or anti missile deflectes ejected from
the aircraft   - is dot going down or up ?? They bar
to the right + I see fully-loaded undercarriages then
'out of the blue' a seering white light comes from nowhere
as if to light them up - to show more of them to me. I so
to myself - they are 'TORNADOES'.   The white ligh

resembles a helicopter search light — but I then say
to myself — it can't be — how can a helicopter be
at the same level, or speed as a plane?

fades to a distance + then as if I get NO PAUSE I go Everything
straight to another scene (Dream 3?)

PICTURES

DISTANT IMAGE
RUNWAY.

SOMETHING BURST OF WHITE LIGHT
AS IF EJECTED OR SHOOTED
UPWARDS   FEELING OF
SOMETHING LIKE ANTI MISSILE
/ IMPACT ...

—LARGE TAIL

LIGHT / LIGHTING
UP IMAGES OF
AIRCRAFT

WEAPON / LOADS

2x
AIRCRAFT

THE
MOON
MAYBE ?)))
(SPIRIT)

ALL DARK / NIGHT TIME

AS I wrote I'm thinking two things Ⓐ 99% sure
that the aircraft represent 2 TORNADOS — A3

THEY ARE AN ENGLISH AIRCRAFT   —   2 DEVASTING
B LOTS OF WEATHER TO HIT UK. (USING THE AMOUNT OF BOMBS
SYMBOLISM → WEAPON LOADS TO INDICATE THE FORCE OF THEM + IT WILL
HAPPEN AT NIGHT
TORNADOES / AIRCRAFT USED IN WAR — e.g. BOSNIA — SARAJEVO   Ⓑ 1%

Tornado ADV

RAF Tornado F3 of No. 111 (Fighter) Squadron

Role	Interceptor
Manufacturer	Panavia Aircraft GmbH
First flight	27 October 1979
Introduction	1 May 1985
Status	Retired
Primary users	Royal Air Force (historical)
	Royal Saudi Air Force (historical)
	Italian Air Force (historical)
Number built	194[1]
Developed from	Panavia Tornado IDS

The Tornado ADV was originally designed to intercept Soviet bombers as they were traversing across the North Sea with the aim of preventing a successful air-launched nuclear attack against the United Kingdom. In this capacity, it was equipped with a powerful radar and beyond-visual-range missiles; however, initial aircraft produced to the F2 standard lacked radars due to development issues. The F3 standard was the definitive variant used by the RAF, the RSAF and the AMI (which leased RAF aircraft).

During its service life, the Tornado ADV received several upgrade programmes which enhanced its aerial capabilities and enabled it to perform the Suppression of Enemy Air Defenses (SEAD) mission in addition to its interceptor duties. Ultimately, both the RAF and RSAF retired their Tornado ADV fleets; the type has been replaced in both services by the Eurofighter Typhoon.

(Source Military Wiki)

Squadron Codes

NQ (Nov 1938 – Sep 1939)
FT (Sep 1939 – May 1947)
SW (Feb 1949 – Apr 1951)
A (Carried on Phantoms)
G (Carried on Tornados)

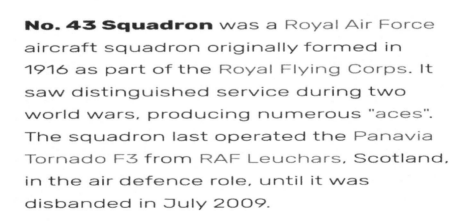

No. 43 Squadron was a Royal Air Force aircraft squadron originally formed in 1916 as part of the Royal Flying Corps. It saw distinguished service during two world wars, producing numerous "aces". The squadron last operated the Panavia Tornado F3 from RAF Leuchars, Scotland, in the air defence role, until it was disbanded in July 2009.

Conclusion: Precognition confirmed 25 days later by television and newspaper reports. Two RAF F3 Tornadoes based in Scotland were on training manoeuvres when they collided 60 miles over the North Sea. Both the pilot and navigator escaped by ejecting from one plane, rescued by helicopter, while the other aircraft got back to base.

So, having read the dream log from 1995, it feels like it was yesterday. And there are some fascinating insights into this 'Precog' because it was as if I'm viewing the action 'scenes' of a film. Having said that, the imagery of something shooting up/ ejecting into the air (which I thought was some sort of missile?) therefore turned out to be an ejector's seat. It was very dark, of course, and everything was happening instantly, but why did I not recognize this? The white dot going up and down was obviously the helicopter searchlight as it hovered above it ... which explains why it appeared to be at the same level/height as the plane. This was definite confirmation, and a perfect (positive) correlation! What's great to know is that the flight crew from both aircraft survived ... hurrah! Finally, no deaths!

I have included my original 1995 dream log/scribbles and drawings above as usual, and for all those aviation fans out there (and because I've loved military aircraft ever since I was a kid), a couple of pictures and some information regarding the F3 Tornado too. And finally on this one, in another ironic personal twist—the two aircraft involved flew out from RAF Leuchars (in Scotland)—which was where I was stationed for 3 months in 1992-93!

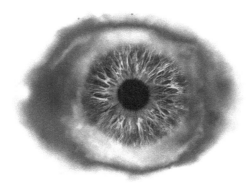

Boy Drowned in a Bath

Method: Lucid Dreams—Wednesday 12 July 1995.

Time before confirmation/evidence/proof: 1 day/10 days—Newspaper articles (13 and 22 July 1995).

Location/ landmarks: House/Bathroom/hospital.

People: Me/ my brother Steve. A young boy. Later a nurse.

Day or Night: Day.

Scene: Bathroom—bath full of water.

Colours: Recall fair coloured hair.

Smells: N/A

Vehicles: N/A

Feelings: Great sadness … and yet joy of love all around.

Dream Log: Wow! So much to recall, one dream followed the other, yet two dreams seemed connected and yet separate which is bizarre. I must have dreamt 3 or 4 times altogether but regarding precognitions concerned, it is like the dimensions of time and space interweave … as if experiencing two events almost simultaneously—if that is even possible? I say this because the imagery received involved a child in both, so could one dream signify events in two different places? Hopefully this will make more sense as you read on.

Copy of original Log—Dream 1. Whether this start was followed on by that very brief piece of info I'm not sure. I'll say this is the start of dream one teaching me.

Characters	Places	Misc.
Me	Bathroom	Leak
Brother Steven		Pipes/water
A child		Drowning

There was a sink in a bathroom. Steven and I were working on the pipes —with some difficulty. There were problems, water started to come out and I said, "Let me see if this makes any difference."

I went to the bath. It was full of water. I'm looking into the water as it drains away. Suddenly … a 'child' seems to come at me, (it's very hard to say this—i.e., with my vision) floating to the surface. It was a boy—about 3? —8 years of age. Fair hair—naked (seemed at first a baby). The name James(?) came to me. You would think this would have shocked me into waking up—but there was a pause.

Somehow the child was at a hospital—I was saying, "Breathe … please breathe." A nurse then said he has a heart problem—valve (?), he'll need another one. Perhaps you could donate, and we could put an artificial one in for you." This took me aback … and I strangely didn't know what to say. I recall the boy's(?) eyes moving and a sound or two from him. I then woke up.

· 2 dreams
both connected

Wed night 12/7/95

WOW!

So much to recall —

PRECOGNITION
100% I'm sure
✓ pto

one dream followed the other

NB

FULL
MOON
TONIGHT

Bed. 10.45 pm
Awoke 6.23 AM — Sleep — Rewoke 8.40 AM

Linked — followed
on

Dream ① *, whether this start was followed on by that
very brief piece of info I'm not sure.   I'll say
this is the start of dream ① - Teaching.

Characters	Places	MISC
Me. —	Bathroom	Leak
Brother Steven		Pipes. Water
A child		— Drowning.

There was a sink in a bathroom.

Steven + I were ~~were~~ working on the pipes – some difficulty.

There were problems.

Water started to come out + I said, "Let me see if this makes any difference."

I went to the bath – it was full of water.

I'm looking into the water as it drains away.

Suddenly – a 'child' seems to come at me (very hard to say this – ie with my vision) Floating to the surface.

It was ~~a~~ boy – about 3? ~~8~~ years of age. Fair hair – naked (seemed at first a baby!)

The name James? – came to me.

You would think this would have shocked me into waking up – but there was a pause and then,

PRECOGNITION! 22/7 report

Somehow the child was at a hospital – I was saying – breathe – breathe... please breathe. A nurse then said he has a heart problem – valve? he'll need another one. Perhaps you could donate and we could put an artificial one in for you. – This took me aback and I (strangely) didn't know what to say.

I recall the boys eyes moving and a sound or two from him.

I then woke up

(MAYBE I WAS ALSO PICKING UP ON ANOTHER PRECOG KIRSTY. FAIR HAIR SEE PAPER AGED 3!! CUTTING)

(NB) – The first thing that came / worried me was James may replace + then I remembered (and I remember falling back asleep as I did so) that mother also had a son called James (Michael's brother). James had a twin that died I'm sure. Confusion – 'James' I saw as a teenager when he came to visit once so why did I think of his 'name' in the drowning??

Bathroom – need to eliminate, cleanse, or take in process of dying so

Sink.

Work

Brother

Precognition

(NB) FACT: LAST NIGHT ON NEWS A BABY GIRL WAS THE YOUNGEST TO HAVE A PACEMAKER FITTED TO HER HEART (SIZE OF THUMBNAIL APX). WAS THIS IN MY SUBCONSCIOUS + STRONG ENOUGH TO PROMPT THIS DREAM? IT WOULD BE A SENSIBLE CONCLUSION BUT IN THIS CASE I DON'T THINK SO!

Water — Spirit / emotions — Clear = purity
Bath

BABY / CHILD   New Consciousness, new awareness —
DROWNING?

HOSPITAL → Contrary dream- good health + feeding of worry (Another death if visit patient

NURSE

OPERATION   ✗ If VISITING PATIENTS IN DREAM
                    DISTRESSING NEWS FROM THE ABSENT ✗

children — Joy feeding spontaneity. One's own inner child
— sometimes abandoned child.

Seems rgt - It felt as if the baby / child was coming into my
very being — into me — my mind — (Connected - as if I went into the
water, and joined as one.

↑
↓

✗ Conclusion ✗
It felt recognition straight away, but no 'newspaper' symbol
A weird feeling — Seeing that baby — child
before me was very strange.   It was like
I was in the water too!   Looking at it, as if it was
infront of my face. / In my head!

BOY, 8, KILLED BY THE HEAT

Tom collapses trying to cool down in bath

By KEVIN LUDDEN

A **BOY** of eight drowned in his bath when he passed out in the heatwave, it was revealed yesterday.

Tragic Thomas Unwin felt drowsy when he came in from riding his bike in scorching temperatures nearing 90F.

His mum Kathleen, 34, put him in a tub to cool him off. But 30 minutes later his horrified dad Michael found him under the water.

Michael, 36, pulled Thomas out and frantically gave him the kiss of life at their home in Doncaster, South Yorks. Neighbour Ken Alderwick said: "If that father could have ripped his own heart out to give his son life he would have."

But the popular little lad, who is thought to have had heat exhaustion, died despite a battle by police, para-

Continued on Page Seven

BOY KILLED

Continued from Page One

medics and hospital staff. Kathleen and Michael, who have two other children Mark, 14, and Jane, 12, were too shattered to talk.

But close family friend Ken, 44, said: "Mick went beyond all means to try to save his boy. He deserves a medal.

"He was crying and choking but he went straight into action."

FUNERAL

Other neighbours immediately took up a street collection to help pay for the animal-loving schoolboy's funeral.

Thomas's big brother Mark sadly offered his savings to the fund.

He said: "It's £10 from my holiday money to go with the £3 from my pocket money. I don't want it any more."

Neighbour Liz Purnell, 44, said: "Thomas was a lovable boy with such a smile that we all fell in love with him. He was

everybody's son."

Police inspector John Townend said: "Thomas's mother says he seemed to perk up after being put in the bath. She gave him soap and left him.

"His father only found him when he went up to see he was OK.

"An eight-year-old is certainly old enough to be left alone in a bath."

An inquest will be opened next week.

Sun doctor Rosemary Leonard said last night: "It's possible Thomas had severe heatstroke.

"Together with dehydration, if he hasn't drunk enough, that can lead to unconsciousness, and he could then have gone under the water."

Heat causes a first

THE Caribbean-style weather caused an exotic plant to bear fruit for the first time in 200 years. A 30ft breadfruit tree at Kew Gardens, West London, has been bare since being brought back from the West Indies by Captain Bligh on the famous HMS Bounty.

Hunt said: "They're all over the curtains and I can't even see the TV screen." An RSPCA ambulance rushed to aid a mother duck and ducklings suffering from heat exhaus... stopping traffic ... Baker Street, Lond...

A pensioner ... robbed by two "... samaritans" after ... collapsed from hea... haustion in **Birmingh**... The two men helped ... 75-year-old back ho... then swiped £100 ... her pension book.

Water chiefs sugge... people with even s... numbers should w... gardens only on o... days of the month,... odds the rest. The p... was a bid to avoid... hosepipe ban in **Kent**...

A massive 13ft sunfl... has been spotted off t... Isle of Wight.

But the heatwa... made no difference ... dairy workers Ma... Wright and Tony Fu... ness from **Norwich**, No... folk — they wo... overcoats and gloves ... stack ice-cream in tem... peratures of -30C.

---

2 EVENING TELEGRAPH, Saturday, July 22, 1995

World today

Saturday

Round-up

● They just love the rail strike!

FILM makers are one group of people delighted by the British Rail strike - it means they can now shoot in railway stations without having to worry about crowds.

... makers of an updated ...

Heatwave death

AN EIGHT-YEAR-OLD boy drowned in his bath after playing in the sweltering heat all day.

Thomas Unwin felt drowsy after riding his bike in temperatures up to 89F.

His 34-year-old mother Kathleen put him in the bath to cool him off from suspected heatstroke at his home in Doncaster, South Yorks.

Police said his mothe... left him in the bath to attend to her othe... children.

Half an hour later h... 36-year-old fathe... Michael found hi... under the water.

West

Evening Telegraph

KIRSTY'S A WORLD BEATER!

by Paul Holmes

YOUNG Kirsty Sanderson has made history by having the world's smallest pacemaker fitted.

It's only the size of a thumbnail and weighs 12.8 grammes but it will play a big part in the youngster's life.

The three-year-old was born with both a hole in her heart and problems with her valves.

She needs the pacemaker to help her heart beat at a normal rate.

Kirsty already had a pacemaker, which was the size of a 50p piece, but need the new one when its battery ran down.

The youngster is now back from Harefield Hospital, Middlesex, after having the new one fitted and old one taken out.

Kirsty's dad Steve Sanderson, 28, of Westfield Avenue, Rushden, said: "She was even running around the day after the operation. Kirsty is just so full of life, she is so determined to survive.

"It is a relief and we are proud she was the first person to have the operation.

"Kirsty is fine although she will have to go back in September for a check-up."

The pacemaker will monitor her heart rate and adapt itself, particularly when she exercises.

Despite its space-age technology it cost just £1,595.

Paediatric cardiologist at Harefield Hospital, Dr Rosemary Radley-Smith, said: "This new little pacemaker has already made a big impact on Kirsty's life.

"It means she will undergo fewer operations and simpler surgery in the future."

When she was only a few weeks old Kirsty had to have an eight-hour operation because of her heart condition.

■ **PICTURE OF HAPPINESS** . . . little Kirsty and, inset, her pacemaker is the size of a thumbnail

Picture by Alan Castle ET picture C/L45640.23a

Conclusion: This was a confirmed precognition case/perfect positive correlation, as you will see from the newspaper articles above. However, it appears two dreams were interconnected because of the last section of my log. It was like I was also picking up on the amazing heart operation with the fair-haired little girl called Kirsty. She had a pacemaker fitted because she had a hole in her heart and problems with her valves. She was aged 3. I mentioned that the young boy's face in the bath (which came right up before my eyes) made me feel he was between 3—8 years of age. He was in fact aged 8, so the age span fitted them both, which is bizarre indeed.

Further within my scribblings, you will see in the pages sidebar the following notes which must have been added the next day? It reads: N.B. FACT—Last night on the TV news that a baby girl was the youngest to have a pacemaker fitted to her heart. (Size of a thumbnail approx.) Was this in my subconscious and strong enough to prompt this dream? It would be a sensible conclusion but, in this case, I don't think so!

One major discrepancy, however, was the young boy's name … I believed it was James, though it was actually Thomas (bless him). In the additional log, when I reflected on the dreams—the first thing that came to me/worried me, was that one of my nephews is James, who was aged 4, with fair hair. I remembered as I was falling back asleep, that my step-mother also had a son called James, whose twin died. Hmm … confusion here though, because I saw James as a teenager when he came to visit once, so why did I think of his name too—in the drowning dream?

Initially the dream symbols threw up the following: Bathroom: the need to eliminate, cleanse, or be in the process of doing so. Water: Spirit/emotions— if clear = purity. Baby/child: new consciousness, new awareness. Hospital: contrary dream, good health, and freedom of worry, or if visiting patients in the dream, it could mean distressing news from the absent. Children: joy, freedom, spontaneity. One's own inner child—sometimes abandoned child.

Perhaps in some small way I was helping the young boy cross over into God's love and light? It felt as if he was coming into my very being, into me, into my mind. We were connected, as if I went into the water and joined as one. It felt like precognition straight away, but this time I received no 'newspaper' symbol or 'key.' A weird feeling indeed. Bless his family, Spirit. Give them all strength and love … at this crossing over of one so, so young. (Karmic?) God's child.

Horse Race Winner

Method: Dream— Monday 16 October 1995.

Time before confirmation/evidence/proof: 13 days—Newspaper articles (28 and 29 October 1995).

Location/landmarks: Horse race winning enclosure?

People: Me.

Day or Night: Day.

Scene: Watching a horse on a screen. Flowers symbols. Name/numbers.

Colours: Golden chestnut.

Smells: N/A

Vehicles: N/A

Feelings: Immediate ... a horse race winner, name OLYMPIA, I think?

Dream Log: Could this be a precognition for me? Suddenly a horse is in my vision. Very large, beautiful racehorse. Its mane being looped, tied. The jockey gets off. A voice says, "It very nearly didn't run as it was found to have been unwell, an infection, a worm in its lining." I had the feeling of OLYMPIA?? (I think).

Suddenly this appeared as if on a large TV screen. There are 6 flowers – HYACINTHS? with numbers 1 to 6. A hand appears above this one ... number 4. (See drawing). The hand gave a wave, as if/like the Queen would move her hand to acknowledge. I felt it was number 4 … AS IF TO SAY THIS ONE. I then had fadeout and woke up.

After this I made some additional notes:

First feeling 4 of 6 = number 4.

Race meeting … OLYMPIA? Queens Horse?

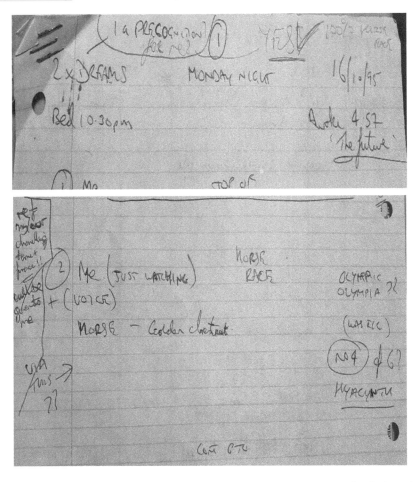

Could the name of the horse be HYACINTH? Mm … don't laugh. I then thought of Channel 4 TV, the comedy programme, 'Keeping up Appearances'. Mrs Bouquet aka MRS BUCKET! He he. This felt so strong, as if I should bet on this horserace.

MONDAY NIGHT. - 16/10/95

Could this be
a precognition for me   YES ⟶ 29/10/95
                                      passed

Suddenly a horse is in my vision. Very large. beautiful
- race horse. It's mane being looped, tied. The
jockey gets off. A voice says, " + it very
nearly didn't run as it was found to have been
unwell - an infection a worm in its timing "!

I had the feeling of OLYMPIA ?? (I think).

                SUDDENLY   THIS APPEARED AS
                IF ON A TV SCREEN

WINNING ENCLOSURE ??

WHITE
RAIL

A HAND
APPEARED
ABOVE THIS
ONE

GOLDEN
CHESTNUT
COLOUR

FLOWERS
A HYACINTH ??

A HAND GAVE A WAVE
& AS IF LIKE THE
QUEEN (would)

MOVE HER HAND TO
ACKNOWLEDGE

I felt
it was
NO ④

POSSIBLY
ON A HAT ON
EACH

⑥
TOTAL

①
②
④
③

AS IF TO SAY ITS THIS ONE

I then had
far out.
          1st feeling   4 of 6   N° 4

Race meeting OLYMPIA?   Dont forget!
                                             thought of
aueens horse ??
Name of the horse HYACINTH.   CHANNEL 4 TV

Also. Comedy Programme "Keeping up Appearances"   MRS BOUQUET (MRS BUCKET)

This felt so strong.

Do if I should bet on this horse / race

To look at for   OLYMPIA. *   ✓   ✓
                  no 4 — winner?   6 HORSE RACE

                  HYACYNTH
                  Mrs BOUQUET ??   ACTUALLY
                                                    NAME TURNED
                                                    OUT
                                                    BE OLYMP

Another angle
To look at this through dream meanings

(NB) — No 4   Master of self + laws of earth. Initiation Sacraf
              Karma as signified by the Cross.
one book
states :-

Horse — Strength, progress — Energy to carry one through.

                              29/10/95 —   OH WELL
                                                 THANKS
                                                 SPIRI
                                                 + MY FRIEND

SORRY. —   AFTER LOOKING OUT FOR

A HORSE CONNECTION FOR THE LAST 12 DAYS
I WENT TO WORK YESTERDAY 28/10/95 10pm —
I DID NOT LOOK AT MEETINGS + HORSES IN A PAPER
+ I THEN MISSED THIS!!

                              — SUNDAYS PAPER

RACE RESULTS
      4·00   OLYMPIAN   GR
      ⇓
4 WAS THE TIME !!   ⇓   ⇓
+ THE   SPOT ON FAVRT   6 RAN
    RUNNING No TOO   (N) on the end   = 6 RUN
                   NAME OF HORSE

And what about looking at this from another angle, through dream 'meanings? One dream dictionary states number 4 is the master of self and laws and death … initiation sacrifice and karma as signified by the cross. And a horse is strength, progress-energy to carry one through, horsepower.

Conclusion: A perfect positive correlation case. Dear, oh dear, oh dear, I feel like I've let spirit down. I am sure I have had many precognitions which I have not recognised, but this is the first of several horse races/winners that I would receive over the years. Now, before you get carried away and think this guy could make a mint here, I have to explain that it's almost like someone can bear witness to an event like this …but not make money from it. After checking horse race details for 11 days, I then forgot to do it! I was soon to discover that with nearly all the 'tips' 'spirit' would give/help me with, I always seemed to miss out, which is entirely my fault!

From the original Log continued: 29/10/1995 SORRY … AFTER LOOKING OUT FOR A HORSE CONNECTION FOR THE LAST 12 DAYS I WENT TO WORK YESTERDAY 28/10/95 1PM, I DID NOT LOOK AT THE MEETING + HORSES IN THE PAPER + THEN I MISSED THIS!!—SUNDAYS PAPER!

RACE RESULTS

'4.00' WAS THE TIME + THE RUNNING NUMBER TOO

NAME OF THE HORSE This turned out to be OLYMPIAN … almost spot on bar the N on the end! 6 RAN … 6 FLOWERS = 6 RUNNERS

OH WELL … THANKS SPIRIT + MY FRIENDS + TEACHERS. On the next three pages are the newspaper clips. At the top of the first two images, we can see DAILY MIRROR (Saturday,28 OCTOBER 1995) and the bottom image is a close up of the race details. The last two images are from 'The Mail on Sunday (Sunday, 29 OCTOBER 1995) with the result … showing a 3-1 winner!

Mirror RACING

THE No 1 SERVICE

RESULTS

ALL six favourites obliged at Wetherby yesterday and had backers celebrating an 18-1 accumulator.

Wind force came from a seemingly hopeless position to land the Harry Wharton Memorial Handicap Chase by 10 lengths under jockey Jamie Railton.

NEWMARKET Good to Firm

WETHERBY Good

BANGOR Good

GREYHOUNDS

SUNDERLAND

KELSO

Mirror 4 Punters Club Voucher 128

GOING: Good to firm.

1.10 — FORESTERS PATHHEAD NOVICES HURDLE 2m 9f 110y

1.40 — LCL PLS NOVICES H'CAP CHASE

WARWICK

GOING: Good to firm.

1.15 — CONDITIONAL JOCKEYS' H'CAP HURDLE 2m

1.45 — BRANDON H'CAP CHASE 2m

NEWSBOY

1.15 WISE STATEMENT, **1.45** NICKLE JOE, **2.20** JAMES PIGG, **2.50** RAFTERS, **3.25** YUBRALEE, **4.00** OLYMPIAN, **4.35** KILCARNE BAY

BOUVERIE

1.15 PUSEY STREET BOY, **1.45** DR ROCKET, **2.20** JAMES PIGG, **2.50** RAFTERS, **3.25** HELLO PETER, **4.00** VICTOR BRAVO, **4.35** MR KERMIT

NORTHERN CORRESPONDENT: **1.15** WORDSMITH, **1.45** CRAFTY CHAPLAIN, **3.25** CONEYGREE

BLINKERS FIRST TIME: Alka International (3.25), Le Sorcier (V- 3.25).
FAVOURITES: 123 have won in 292 races, an average of 42.1%.
TELEVISION: All races covered live on SIS.

4.00 — BONUSPRINT NOVICES' CHASE
2m 4f 110y £3,866 (6 run)

1	315-	Cracking Idea (169)	J Edwards 7 11 0		D Bentley	—
2	6/P/	Greybury Star (623)	K Bailey 7 11 0		T J Murphy	—
3	00-	Master Hunter (194)	J White 6 11 0		D Bridgwater	—
4	003-	Olympian (194)	(B) Mrs L Murphy 8 11 0	(C, F)	M Richards	31
5	5/2-	Take Chances (330)	Mrs P Dutfield 7 11 0		B Powell	30
6	2/4-	Victor Bravo (NZ) (364)	N Gaselee 8 11 0	(SF)		
					J R Kavanagh	32

Betting: 6-4 Olympian, 11-4 Victor Bravo, 7-2 Cracking Idea, 11-2 Take Chances, 16 Greybury Star, Master Hunter.

4.35 — BONUSPRINT NATIONAL HUNT FLAT RACE 2m £1,350 (12 run)

1	10	Tipping The Line (22)	M Pipe 5 11 11	(D, SF)	*O Burrows

RACING

Pearl's a winner

Oxx filly is Mile queen

From Laurie Brannan
in New York

IRISH-TRAINED filly Ridgewood Pearl ran the race of her life to win the Breeders' Cup Mile at rain-soaked Belmont Park yesterday.

Britain's Sayyedati, running her last race, finished third, and the other home-trained runner Soviet Line a remote sixth.

Sayyedati, whose career wins included the One Thousand Guineas and the Sussex Stakes, was bidding to give Clive Brittain his 1,000th winner.

Ridgewood Pearl, who was bred in England, may also have run her last race, said trainer John Oxx.

Draped in the Irish flag, her colourful owner Sean Coughlan, famous for his post-race victory parties, said: 'She was brilliant today. Other sports have their world cups — it was ours.'

Jockey Johnny Murtagh described the win as the greatest moment of his career. He said: 'It feels so good to come back and prove she's the best in Europe. It was unbelievable.'

Sayrayir was withdrawn having injured her near-hind at exercise on Friday.

Britain's big guns failed to fire in the Breeders' Cup event. Frankie Dettori was unable to put up a big challenge on Tamure in the early stages of the race, but the Geoff Wragg-trained colt faded to finish seventh behind the winner, Desert Stormer.

'We were a bit slow out of the box and he got tired in that last half furlong,' said Dettori.

Chief Golf Rose, one of the most improved fillies in training — she has won races in five different countries this year — finished eighth. 'She jumped off well, but faded in the straight and did not kick on at the end,' said jockey Jason Weaver. Undaunted, rookie trainer Joe Naughton, so pleased but to have a runner, went ahead with his planned party in Manhattan last night.

Groove

Lake Coniston failed to overcome a bad draw and beat only one of the 13 runners. Pat Eddery appeared to use him up to get a good position early in the race. Eddery said he broke all right and I had a good position until the turn, but he got a little dirt in his face and that was it.'

Dettori was also out of luck on Tamure, who could finish only fourth behind Northern Spur in the Breeders' Cup Turf. He was a bit keen early on. He then relaxed and found a groove in the back straight and got close. He had every chance.

The biggest disappointment of the day was Halling in the Breeders' Cup Classic. The winner of his last eight races, he finished stone last behind America's horse of the year, Cigar, for whom it was business as usual, completing his 12th consecutive win.

POST HASTE . . . Johnny Murtagh on Ridgewood Pearl pulls away from Fastness to win the Breeders' Cup Mile

Bank jumps in style

By Charles Lewis

BARTON BANK, who threw away last season's King George VI Chase at Kempton when unshipping Adrian Maguire at the final fence, is on course for the Boxing Day showpiece after scoring at Wetherby yesterday.

David Nicholson's 8-15 shot jumped faultlessly to slam Young Hustler in the Charlie Hall Chase.

Owner Jenny Mould praised Ginny Elliot, the three-day eventer, for the improvement in Barton Bank's jumping.

Mrs Mould said: 'I love my horse but he almost gives me heart failure! I decided to send Barton Bank to Ginny for some extra tuition and it appears to have worked.'

Ginny added: 'He had lost his confidence so we decided to start from scratch.'

Star to point the way

By Laurie Brannan

DATO STAR, despite not winning so far this season, looks the likely favourite for the last big Flat race of the year, Doncaster's Tote November Handicap on Saturday.

Already 8-1 with the sponsors, he owes his position to three highly-impressive victories in National Hunt Flat races last season, including one at the Cheltenham Festival. But Malcolm Jefferson, his trainer, will be anxiously watching the weather forecast during the next few days. The Malton handler said yesterday: 'He is a much better horse on softish ground.'

Dato Star is an exciting hurdles prospect, but Jefferson has been unable to school him because of the firm ground.

He added: 'At least he is fit. He had a race at Doncaster last weekend, but it was a pretty rough affair and he never really got a run.'

Seckar Vale, owned by Jack Hanson, who has already won the race twice, looks the danger.

John Dunlop, who clinched a popular win with his first trainers' championship last weekend, can click with both Serendipidy, on Friday, and Captain Horatius, on Saturday, at Doncaster.

TIPS OF THE WEEK

TOMORROW: Donna Aroma, Bev Heath Boy (Newcastle), Palm Creek, Call Me Ada (Plumpton).

TUESDAY: Kalamata, Saxende (Sedgefield, Marina's Dan Chester).

WEDNESDAY: Dublow Lodge (Kempton), Spanish Light (Haydock), Power Stake (Newton Abbot).

THURSDAY: Ameria, Minguette (Edinburgh).

FRIDAY: Serendipidy, Aughere, No Monkey Nuts (Doncaster).

SATURDAY: Dato Star, Tazrila, Captain Horatius (Doncaster).

RESULTS

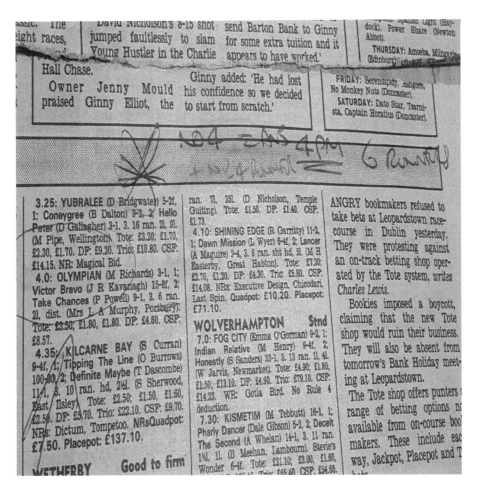

Like I've said before … never look a gift horse in the mouth! What a
numpty head!

PRECOGNITION 14

My Big Lottery Win (Not)

Method: Dream—Tuesday 31 October 1995.

Time before confirmation/evidence/proof: 34 days—Newspaper 3 December 1995.

Location/landmarks: Home/stairs/hall-landing area.

People: Me/Caroline.

Day or Night: Night.

Scene: Holding a lottery ticket 4 numbers.

Colours: Black and white.

Smells: N/A

Vehicles: N/A

Feelings: Elation at winning.

Dream Log: This was about lottery numbers, and I awoke at 4.52 a.m. … my mind racing. (As always, as per my original notes further below).

I had a lottery ticket in my hand— "We'd won!" I shouted. I ran up the stairs … Caroline came out of the bathroom, with only her pants and bra on, and cleaning her teeth. "What? How many numbers?" she asked. (As we met at the top of the stairs) The ticket was in front of me. I said,

"There's the 4 numbers—3 £10 numbers. That one makes 5." (Or did I say would have made 5?) NB. Something about £100? £100? £100,000?) I began circling the numbers and I woke up!!

Now then, this immediately happened … I could NOT recall the numbers—everything … the ticket was a blur. Why? How? (4 weeks ago, I had 6 numbers in a dream—I remembered them clearly—and 2 weeks ago, 33 + 21 came out … not enough to win £10! I lay awake for ages … fifteen plus minutes just thinking—closing my eyes—no recall!

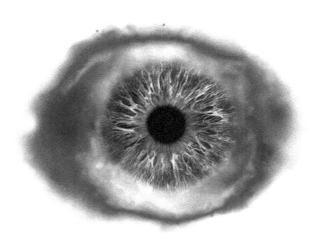

① 4 NO'S IN LOTTERY DREAM
CORRECT

<u>TUESDAY NIGHT</u>   1 x DREAM   31/10/95

⟨50%⟩ → £00 % ✲

This was about Lottery numbers

woke 4.52   —   My mind racing.

I had a lottery ticket in my hand — (we'd won) I shouted
I ran up the stairs
Cochine came out of the bathroom, pants + Bra only on
cleaning her teeth
"what ?? "How many numbers?" she asked as we met at
at the top of the stairs.
    The ticket was in front of me
    I said — There's the 4 numbers — 3 t10 numbers
    That one makes 5   (or did I say would have made
    5 ?
    ⟨NB⟩   Something about £00 — £00 ? £100,000 ?? ??

    I began circling the <u>numbers</u> + I <u>woke up</u>!!

Now then, immediately this happened... I could <u>NOT</u> recall
    the numbers —   anything — the ticket was a Blur.

why? How?!   ⟨NB⟩ 4 weeks ago I had 6 numbers in a dream — remember
then clearly — 2 weeks ago 33, +21 come out — not enough
to win a £10 —
                    I lay awake for ages 15+ mins
just thinking — closing my eyes —   no recall !

Then I thought of Spirit ... Yes, vibrations came. If I
go through the numbers ~ ~ ~   A 'yes' vibration was then
given for   7, 16, 19, 26, 28, 29

I then asked if was this week ⟨NO⟩ + the yes vibration came
after <u>4 weeks</u> —   I will use these numbers too...
— IS IT my DESTINY ?!

⟨NB⟩ After 4 weeks passed 28/11/95 → the next sat no 2/12/95
4 NO'S came up.   16 19 26 being the 1st 3 balls
drawn. — No 7 was the BONUS NUMBER £10 WON   PTO

Then I thought of Spirit … 'Yes' vibrations were then given for numbers 7, 16,19,26,28,29. (NB. I receive what I call 'energy pulses' like a brrrrr,brrrr,brrrr sound/feeling in my ears … right ear for 'yes' … left ear for 'no)'. I then asked if this was for this week … 'No'. And the 'yes' vibrations came after 4 weeks. I will use these numbers too … IS IT MY DESTINY?

After 4 weeks had passed (28/11/95) … the next Saturday was 2/12/94 and 4 numbers came up. 16,19,26 being the first 3 balls drawn … number 7 was the <u>BONUS</u> NUMBER. <u>£10 WON</u>   PTO

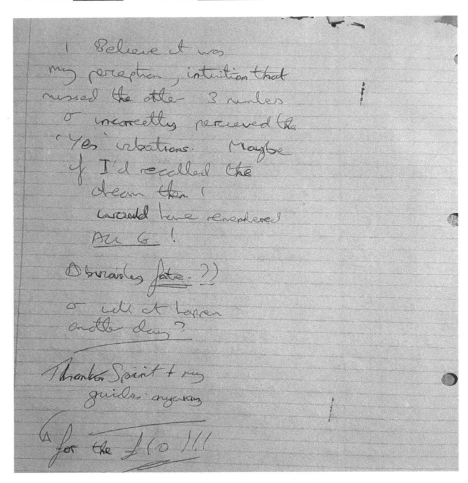

Conclusion: At first when I looked back on this and the lottery results, I thought about stating this as a weak to moderate correlation. However, it clearly mentions 4 numbers —3 '£10 numbers' in the first paragraph, so I am saying it has a strong predictive validity its initial meaning. Spirit never wastes energy in trying to support and guide us in our lives and often it is our own perceptions which cause errors. Therefore, the 4 numbers are correct. And the 3 refers to the 3 numbers which provide the £10 win! It is important to remember we are all given what we need in life and not necessarily what we think we want. Sai Baba (an avatar of our age), once referred to the following words ... 'I WANT PEACE', stating the I—is our ego, WANT—is our desire ... and if we remove these two, we will be left with PEACE. So, although £100,000 would have been absolutely amazing, I am grateful for the £10 spirit! As my sister always says ... "It's better than a poke in the eye with a blunt stick!"

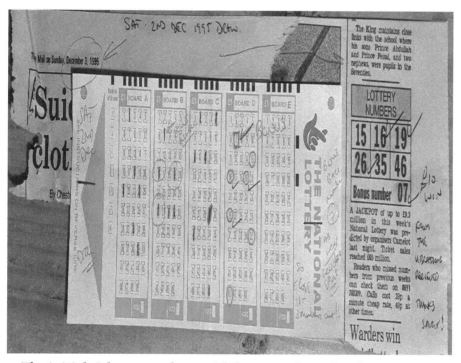

The initial ticket entry form with lotto results + dated newspaper.

I tried again the next 2 weeks using the same numbers, but as you can see in the ticket and newspaper clipping result above, only 2 numbers came up both times! Oh well, if you're not in it you can't win it, they say!

SAT 16TH AGAIN - 2 NUMBERS EMERGED FROM THAT DREAM

The Mail on Sunday, December 17, 1995

EA SC   5

LAST NIGHT'S LOTTERY

| 07 | 08 | 23 |
| 28 | 35 | 49 |

Bonus number 10

STRESSED: Faldo is planning a family Christmas

SPARKLING: Close-up of Brenna Cepelak's diamond and sapphire ring   Picture: TIM CORNELL

Linda McCartney in cancer scare

By Nick Buckley and Paul Nathanson

LINDA McCartney has undergone an operation to remove a lump from her breast, it was revealed last night.

The 53-year-old wife of former Beatle Paul McCartney had surgery six days ago after a routine scan revealed the growth.

McCartney, who lost his mother, Mary, to cancer when he was 14, said the operation had been a complete success.

Linda had a scan at the Princess Grace Hospital in London last week and she was found to have a small lump in her breast,' he said. 'She has had an operation to remove it,

which was performed successfully last Monday. Luckily it was caught in time.'

Linda, a mother-of-four, is a committed vegetarian and runs a hugely successful vegetarian foods empire. Earlier this year she said: 'Doctors say you're far less likely to die of cancer or heart disease if you don't eat meat.' Surgeons are

believed to be confident that they have removed the threat of cancer. But they will not be able to rule out the possibility of Linda having to undergo chemotherapy or radiotherapy until she has further tests in the New Year.

McCartney appealed for his wife to be allowed to recuperate in peace at their farm in Rye, East Sussex.

tary Clare Short claimed that more and more Tory MPs would get cold feet and back off 'as they are asked to defend the indefensible'.

THE National Lottery jackpot was an estimated £9.2 million in last night's draw, with total prizes of £39.2 million.

Organisers Camelot said £30 million from previous draws was still waiting to be claimed. Prizes unclaimed after 180 days are given to 'good causes' — Camelot has donated £20 million so far.

● Readers who missed previous weeks' numbers can check them on 0891 700308. Calls cost 39p a minute cheap rate, 49p at other times.

Lottery Watchdog — Page 6

Grand Prix Crash

Method: Dreams—Wednesday, 1 November 1995 and Monday, 6 November 95.

Time before confirmation/evidence/proof: 9 and 5 days—Newspaper 10 Novemeber 1995 and TV reports.

Location/landmarks: Airfield/ racing track.

People: Men/ single man looked like an Alien!

Day or Night: Day/sunny.

Scene: Accident ... vehicle/object on its side.

Colours: Black and white/green

Smells: N/A

Vehicles: Racing Cars.

Feelings. Flying/watching from above... witnessing a strange suited 'man' (?), panic with group of men running. Sense of being abroad.

Overview: Some of this is going to sound downright absurd and with my horrendous scribbled blurred notes (and the fact that two dreams seemed linked over 5 days apart will seem to confuse the matter further.

Nothing surprises me anymore though, especially after all the lucid dreams, astral projection, and OBE's (out of body experiences) and my bearing witness to different planes and dimensions! Tonight, I feel as if

I'm in a parallel universe of Area 51 and an episode of wacky races. And It's like the dream almost repeats itself! Well, here goes...

Dream Log: 1/11/95 Dream two of the night: Now, unless you imagine we're going to be invaded by aliens, you're going to have to bear with me. Me watching … viewing as flying above. Bizarrely this feels like an alien landing/ship

There is a track, like an airfield. Cars? Large racing 'about' area. Feeling of somewhere abroad. A vehicle? A truck (?)goes off the road/ corner. There's an object on its side.15—20 men run to the scene. Weird feeling of American soldiers. Have 'weapons'/armed rifles? Me thinking it looks like manoeuvres, but they are acting a bit <u>weird</u>.

This place seems like a public 'show' for cars. I'm in a ditch, submerged 'water'? There's a winch (lift car out). A man all green gets out. Weird shape and eyes!! Looks like the HULK but thinner. I have a feeling of 'feeling sorry' for it … being chased, hunted down? Alien? NO HAIR. All green, large … almost bulbous eyes. Some of the green (skin?) seems to be fading … dying? Was standing up though. (Survived)

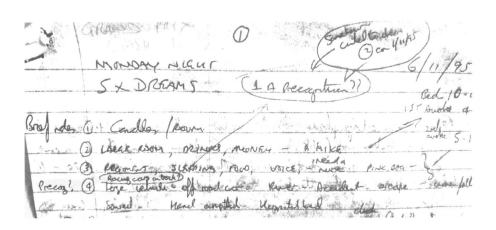

WAS A TRACK

Dream ② PIC 5

1/1/95
TUNNEL DUE TO BE RE EXTINGUISHED

CRASH PLCN WARD BEND

ROAD ??

here — men running, carried rifles ??

?? OBJECT over on its side

TURNED OUT TO BE A CAR

used out to

Telnet

Something wriggled out of ditch ??

— men soldier?

MY PERCEPTION

WAACH

later ??

Something green

ALIEN?? nothing

ALL Green. Large almost
Bulls eyes. — Some of green (skin)
seemed to be fading.

dying ???

WAS STANDING UP TURN 94

One dream book says/suggests
= Alien = foreigner —

RACING DRIVER

MIKA HAKKINEN

Shrunk

SEE PICTURES AT BACK

② Me watching   Airfield   Cars? Large racing 'about' area
                                 an area ?? / track ??

                   A vehicle / truck?   One goes over on its side

ABROAD feeling of
Amarican Soldiers? —   15-20 able to move me

              have weapons?   thinking it looks like 'invasion' x

                              but there acting a bit weird

forget   ← (if it's a public 'show' for cars)
feeling of Aircraft landing
Ships   (or I'm a ditch submerged (water?))

                              Vehicle (Lift cool) out. x

Looks like UKULA but thunder   Men all Green get out
feeling of feeling sorry for 'it' - Being chased   Weird shape + eyes !!
                    hunted down !!

6/11/95 Dream four of the night: Me watching from high above. Precognition? I'm going over a Grand Prix grid … racing cars all on the lines … but some cars missing ... as if not ready yet. Feeling of abroad.

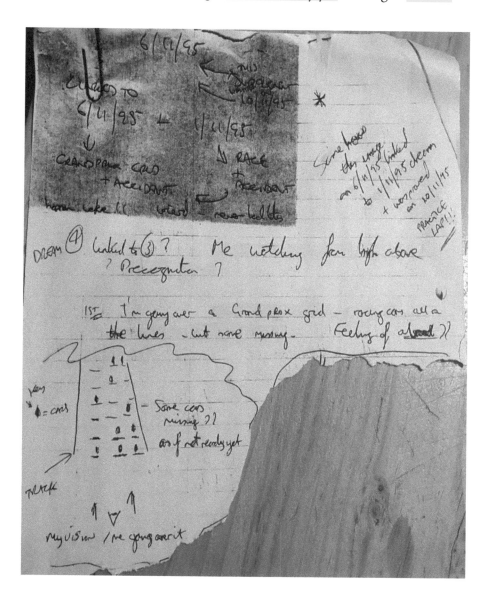

World today

Handwritten annotations: 1/4/95 + 6/11/95 BOTH HAVE THESE; 6/11/95; 1+6/11/95

IN BRIEF

French get a cool reception

POLICE were today protecting French warships visiting Britain against possible protests by environmental campaigners.

A flotilla of French navy vessels sailed up the Thames and docked in London on a "goodwill" visit, to jeers from a handful of protesters.

Meanwhile Commonwealth nuclear testing issued a French hitting statement.

With Britain dissenting, leaders of the 52-strong group meeting in Auckland, New Zealand, said the tests had caused widespread anger and urged their immediate cessation.

Suspect bomb

IRISH police today arrested two men and seized a suspect bomb in a van near the border with Northern Ireland.

The men were arrested at Carrickmacross, Co Monaghan.

One of the men was being held at Dundalk Police station. The other was detained in Carrickmacross.

Both were being held under anti-terrorism laws.

Cancer link

YOUNG athletes taking anabolic steroids run the risk of cancer, doctors warned today.

The claim came after two 26-year-old bodybuilders using the drugs developed kidney cancer. Muscle-building steroids have already been tied to heart disease and impotence.

Yasser visit

YASSER Arafat has visited Israel for the first time to console the widow of assassinated Prime Minister Yitzhak Rabin.

Palestine Liberation Organisation chairman Mr Arafat spent 90 minutes at the Tel Aviv home of grieving Leah Rabin after staying away from Mr Rabin's funeral for security reasons.

Leek Ness!

JAPANESE scientists claim to have discovered a prehistoric monster in a Welsh lake.

The experts said they had captured on film The Beast of Bala Lake – dubbed Leek Ness – as it swam on the surface in Gwynedd.

Prickly rescue

A FIRE crew made an emergency rescue yesterday – when a baby hedgehog got his nose stuck in a cage.

Five firemen cut Tony the hedgehog free from his pen in Holt, Norfolk, after owner Margaret English heard him squealing for help.

£1 for the loo

CUSTOMERS at top people's store Harrods in London are having to pay £1 to spend a penny.

The department store's deluxe toilets boast marble floors, mahogany seats and brass taps.

Grand Prix star in 110mph crash

RACING driver Mika Hakkinen was in serious but stable condition in hospital today after crashing heavily during opening qualifying for the Australian Grand Prix in Adelaide.

A spokesman for the Royal Adelaide Hospital said the 27-year-old Finn was in intensive care with head injuries.

He was being kept under sedation and breathing through a respirator.

The spokesman said Hakkinen's injuries were not life-threatening, but added: "Clearly he is in a serious condition. This is a serious head injury and we will be resting him totally in an intensive care environment and watching his progress closely."

The doctor added it was too soon to say whether Hakkinen would be able to make a full recovery and race again.

Hakkinen lost control of his McLaren on entry to the high-speed Brewery Corner then hit a kerb, launching into the air before slamming backwards into the barriers.

The corner, a fast right-hander between the Jones and Brabham straights, is the quickest on the track and it is believed Hakkinen was travelling at about 110mph when he smashed into the barriers, which are protected by only one wall of tyres.

He was surrounded by emergency medical staff as treatment was carried out trackside. The session

■ CRASH VICTIM . . . Finland's Mika Hakkinen is assisted from the wreckage of his McLaren today.

was red-flagged to a halt for 42 minutes.

When qualifying resumed, Damon Hill grabbed provisional pole position in his Williams ahead of team-mate and fellow-Briton David Coulthard, Austrian Gerhard Berger in a Ferrari and newly-crowned double world champion Michael Schumacher in his Benetton.

Hakkinen's team-mate Mark Blundell took the decision to continue qualifying and ended the session ninth fastest.

Today's accident was the worst in the sport this year.

Japan's Ukyo Katayama escaped with only slight injuries after his Tyrrell car overturned at the start of the Portuguese Grand Prix in September and Japan's Aguri Suzuki suffered a fractured rib in practice for the Japanese Grand Prix at Suzuka last month.

In 1994, at the San Marino Grand Prix at Imola, Austrian Roland Ratzenberger in a Simtek and three-times world champion Ayrton Senna of Brazil, driving a Williams, were killed on successive days in crashes.

On This Day

- **1871** Henry Stanley, sent out to Africa to find missionary David Livingstone, finally made contact with him at Ujiji with the now immortal worlds 'Dr Livingstone, I presume.'
- **1960** On Penguin's first run of D H Lawrence's Lady Chatterley's Lover, all 200,000 copies were sold out on the first day of publication.
- **1982** Soviet president Leonid Brezhnev died aged 75.
- **1988** Thirteen men were rescued from the North Sea after their Sikorsky S61 helicopter was forced to ditch with mechanical failure.
- **1991** Publisher Robert Maxwell was buried Jerusalem 1995 cancel engager

Nov 10 Fri

TODAY'S BIRTHDAYS
- Roy Scheider, actor pictured, 60
- Screamin' Lord Sutch, would-be Prime Minister
- Tim Rice, lyricist, 51

Here's a closer shot of the paper clipping from 10 NOVEMBER 1995 and some links to the crash for the F1 fans.

MIKA HAKKINEN AUSTRALIAN GRAND PRIX CRASH '95

https://www.foxsports.com/stories/motor/twenty-years-on-mika-hakkinen-reflects-on-1995-adelaide-crash

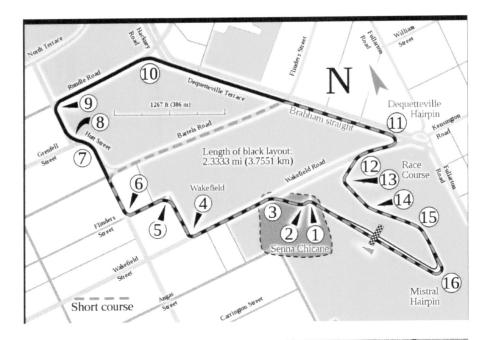

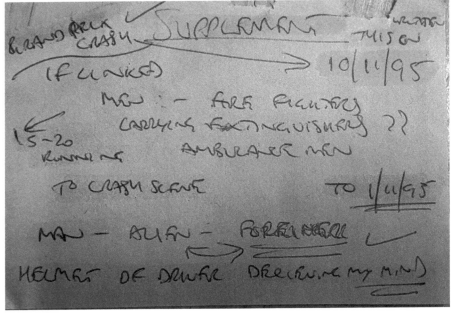

Conclusion: Goodness knows what the Alien angle was in all this! Like in my log/notes above ... it could have represented a clue to the nationality i.e., a foreigner? Maybe the colour green represented the surrounding grass of the track ... and the bald head compared with a driver's helmet? Also, the men looked like they were carrying something like weapons, but could this simply have been pointing fire extinguishers while running towards the car in case it caught fire?

There was nothing to do with water or winches in the newspaper report, though, which is a big miss. Me flying over the grid is spot on with some cars missing though ... perhaps this was the start of the practice / qualifying laps that were mentioned?

Of course, all this could be just me ... whist walking/flying in my sleep, I may have ventured into Ridley Scott's next Alien sci-fi movie set ... Alien vs Grand Prix car's part 1?

What becomes clear is that I must continue to trust in the process and continue this 'spiritual' work ... after all, 'God' does not make mistakes. Like all of us, our perceptions of what we bear witness to can, and will, vary greatly. One could compare this scenario with Chinese whispers. I'll have to keep focused, because I feel there will be greater amounts of symbolism within my future precognition cases than before. So, overall ... perhaps this is a case with moderate correlation? I'll let you be a judge of that.

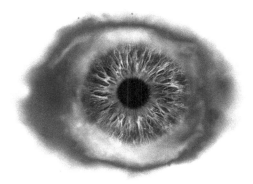

Men's Australian Open Winner

Method: Dream—Wednesday 15 November 1995.

Time before confirmation/evidence/proof: 11 days—Teletext TV

Location/landmarks: N/A but am hunting for books/maps on shelves!

People: Me, my dad.

Day or Night: Night.

Scene: House … shelves/books chair, newspaper picture of golfer.

Colours: White.

Smells: N/A

Vehicles: N/A

Feelings: 4 or more dreams … precognition, hearing a voice talking to me/us (Clairaudience).

Dream Log: I go to bed at 11.20 p.m. During the night I have 4 or more dreams and feel one or more are precognitions. Copy of original notes.

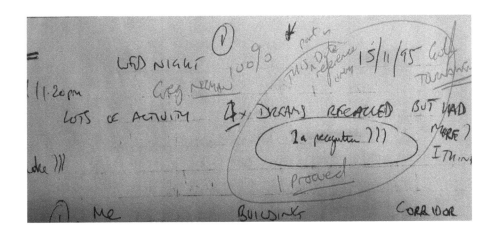

Me		HouseChair
Dad	Newspaper …	MY KEY IN --------
Newspaper	I rip out picture	Golf man
		Malcolm White Hair misheard

Precognition???

WINNER of GOLF tournament   NORMAN (Greg

Me and dad—in a room. There's information given to me/us about a Golf tournament, I hear a voice say the winners name? Malcolm— (But upon waking up I felt I misheard it). I go to a room—shelves jam packed. I was looking for a book, map? Atlas? — "Sorry dad, can't find it." Back to living room … dad is in a chair. There is a newspaper, I rip out the picture of a golfer taking a swing. (See drawing in notes of … Head ½ down right to left swing in picture). There is a date given 25/11/95 or 20/11/95. NORMAN – GREG (Malcolm)

Cont.

First thought … I need to look to lookout for this … + also give info to dad. Bet to win some cash??

I must say that I'm not 100% sure of the name and don't feel it's quite as clear cut as the 'horse' winner the other week.

I feel it's a definite precog though – We shall see!!

(5) * from over. just had started to write that line — Bang — straight into my head. Dream / after 'teaching'

me   House   Chair   ⟨MY KEY IN⟩
Dad   X newspaper X

recognition ???   Golf man
                    ⟨newspaper   Malcolm   ⟨white hair⟩
inner of Golf tournament   I rip out   ↓ ↘ mistaken
                     picture⟩   ↗
                                            NORMAN (Greg.

me + dad — in a room — There's information   ↗ shelfs ⟨MAPS can't find⟩
   given to me / us about a Golf tournament ✓
(I hear a voice say the winners name) ✓
Malcolm (but upon waking I felt I misheard   NORTH (SCOTLAND)
it)   I go to a room — shelves
jam packed — I was looking for a book   Date. 25/11/95 X
map? atlas?? — "Sorry dad, can't find it "   or 20/11/95
back to living room. Dad in a chair
There's a newspaper — I rip out the picture of a golfer taking
   a swing   .   ⟨NORMAN — Greg (Malcolm?⟩
                              ↑ cart

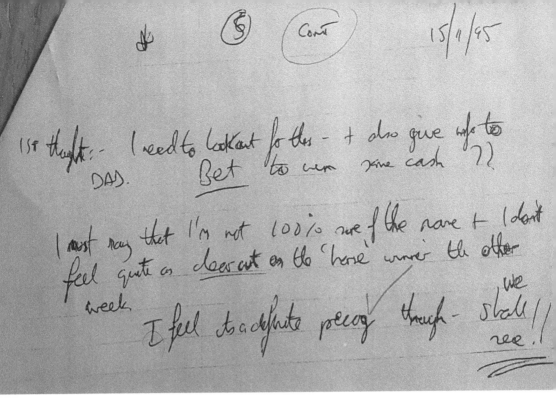

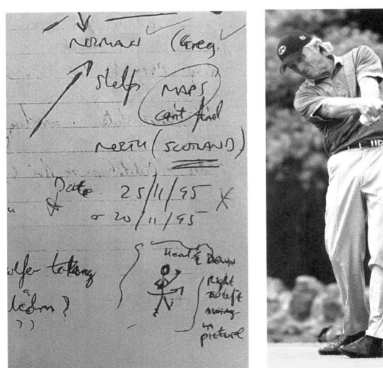

A picture of Greg Norman's swing.
(Credits- Allstar Picture Ltd / Alamy Stock Photos)

photos of Teletext proof ✓

Date of event etc

Name ✓

Golf ✓

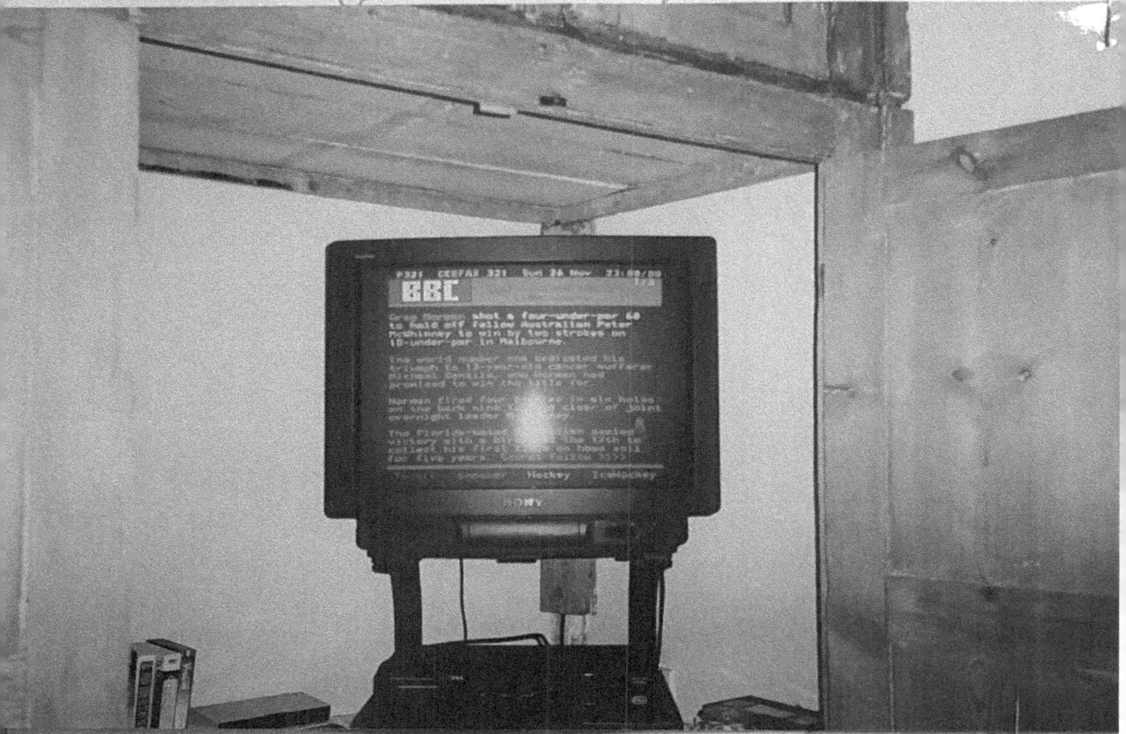

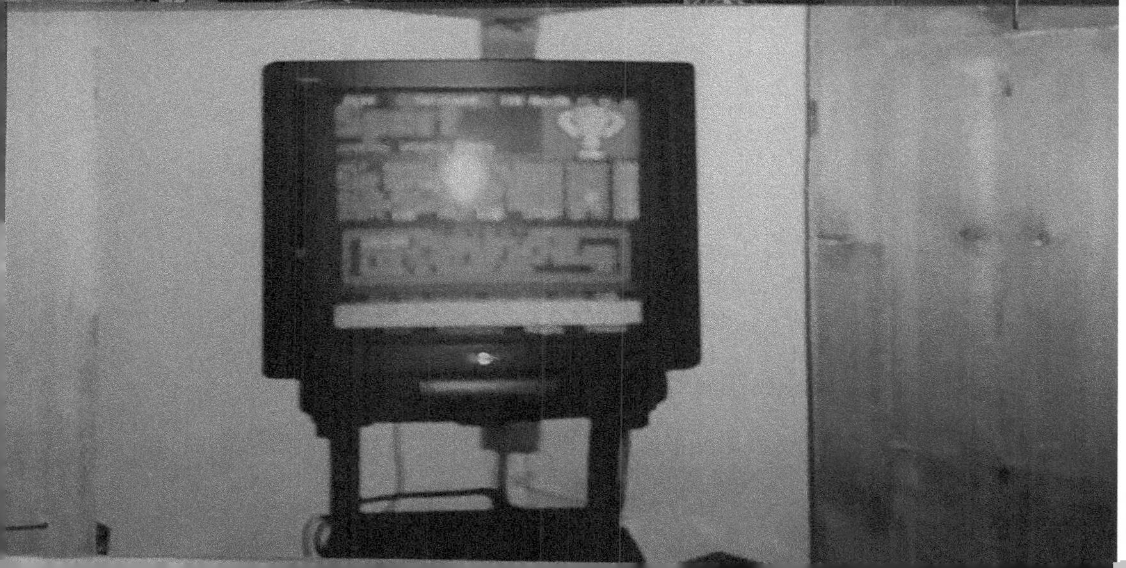

Here are pictures of my old Sony TV back in the day ... goodness knows what happened to the lower image ... me not focusing, dear me!

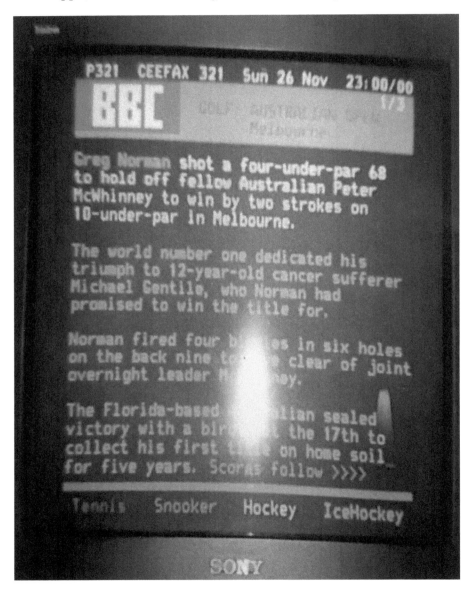

Conclusion: Dear me ... I am a numpty head again! Talk about missed opportunities. The voice even told me the golfer's name. I receive the symbols and messages and even a picture for heaven's sake ... and did I put a bet on .... no! How much evidence or proof do/will I ever need? It's not like I don't trust my 'spirit guides' or God ... so why do I doubt myself? I mean ... white-haired golfer, a voice telling me the winner's name. I even have one of my precognitions 'keys' to verify it—a newspaper. All I had to do was to check when the next tournament was due. My guides must have been tearing their hair out at me ... "Oh Yee of little faith!" Sorry to all concerned! And even worse is that I forgot to tell my dad about this case with a perfectly positive correlation too.

For golf fans out there, here's a wealth of information about Greg Norman aka 'The Shark', https://en.wikipedia.org/wiki/Greg_Norman ... enjoy!

Tamil Tigers Battle of Jaffna

Method: Lucid Dream—Saturday, 25 November 1995.

Time before confirmation/evidence/proof: 10 and 11 days—Newspaper reports.

Location/landmarks: An open area, hills, and mountains nearby.

People: Me, men fighting, shooting.

Day or Night: Night.

Scene: Shooting/fighting going on all over the place.

Colours: Orange.

Smells: N/A

Vehicles: Tank, Land Rover type vehicle, army truck (?)

Feelings: 4 dreams last night … 1 precognition, symbolism really notched up a level in this one! Me watching/viewing and then I am participating, it's like I am in another person's body shooting. Mayhem.

Dream Log: Saturday night 25th Nov 1995. Original notes a mess!

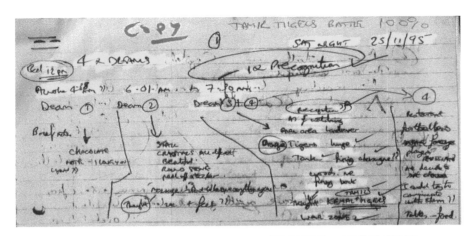

SAT NIGHT 25/11/95

Bed 12pm.

Awoke 4.38 am??

1 x Precognition

6.01am + 7.30am
Dreams (3) + 4
Precognition?
As if watching
Open area ... land rover
Orange, Tigers   huge
Tank ... firing, chasing me?
Woods ... me
firing back

TAMIL
Thought   KEMAL   TIGERS

(3) Felt like precognition
Me 'watching' – as if there and then being/participating.
Jungle, forests, clearing. Going along – Movement in land rover? Vehicle.
Up ahead – hills.   Orange areas – What the??
Staring ... orangutang figures – NO – TIGERS   HUGE
They seemed to come down from the mountain

Suddenly to my left a tank – looming <u>closer</u> ... its turret starting to
wing towards me – '<u>my VISION</u>'
I thought ... 'I'm a <u>friend</u>'   What's this.
I tried to speed up.

Machine gun fire—Pause—Me hiding.

IN WOODS,
JUNGLE or
FOREST

behind a tree—Gun fire towards me ... Needed to
'defend'. I leaned around a tree and started to fire back
towards where the fire had come from.

Then fadeout. 1st thought   Jungle fighting
–KEMEL TIGERS   JUNGLE FIGHTS
MERCENARIES,   KILLERS,   HOSTAGE   TAKERS
TAMIL!!
SHOULD BE

FUNNY
KEMEL
IS THE
NAME
OF OUR
NEXT DOOR
NEIGHBOUR

HILLS   MOUNTAINS
MY DRAWING IS ON THE
ORGINAL LOG SHEET
BELOW

TANK
CAME   FROM   LEFT
ORANGE

BLOBS
BUT THEN TIGERS

③ felt like (precognition)

Me 'watching' – as if there + then being/participating

Jungle, forests clearing. Going along – Movement
in Landrover >1 vehicle.
Up ahead – hills – Orange areas – What the ??
staring – orangutang figures – NO – 'TIGERS' HUGE
They seemed to come down
from the mountain.

Suddenly to my left a tank – looming closer its
turret starting to swing towards me – MY VISION
I thght 'I'm a friend' whats this –
                              I tried to speed

up.   Machine gun fire –   Pause –   me hiding
behind a tree – Gun fire towards me   –   Needed
to 'defend' –   I leaned around & + started to fire
back towards where the fire had geo come from

IN
WOODS,
JUNGLE or
FOREST

Then fade out.   1ST thght :   Jungle fighting
– KEMEL TIGERS – JUNGLE FIGHTS
                  MERCENARIES, KILLERS, HOSTAGE TAKE

FUNNY
KEMEL
IS THE
NAME OF
OUR
NEXT DOOR
NEIGHBOUR

↓TAMIL !!

(SINHL)
TBR

HILLS ← MOUNTAINS

TANK →
CAME FROM
LEFT

ME

ORANGE
BLOBS
BUT THEN TIGERS

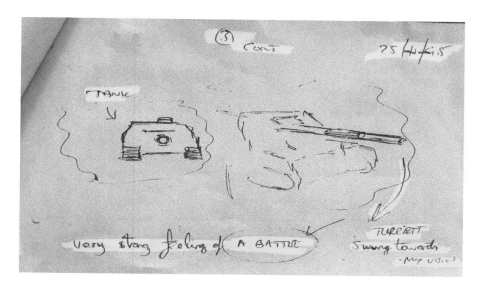

I found this image online (12-3-22) from the conflict ... looks pretty accurate from 27 years ago I'd say!

THE WORLD
THIS WEEK
NOV 1995

NDTV
#25

last night. Ten Labour rebels voted against Mr Clarke's 1p income tax cuts, defying party orders to abstain.

Tamils strike

SRI Lankan Tamil Tiger rebels killed 23 police commandos after the army seized control of the rebels' former stronghold of Jaffna. The commandos died when rebels launched a revenge attack on a police camp .

Conclusion: Wow ... what strikes me with this case is the imagery and symbolism. Sometimes I get this wrong ... but hey ... I mean, orange blobs turning into orangutans (which is a reference to both the colour orange and 'guerrillas') then into tigers. The orange blobs looking like 'JAFFA' cakes (biscuits) ... must represent the town of JAFFNA in Sri Lanka. I'd think it was funny if it wasn't such a serious case. It just goes to show that 'spirit' will use every means possible to convey the truth and have a sense of humour towards me too!

Then there was the ferocious fighting with machine guns which was horrendous, and with the feeling I was in someone else's body was totally bizarre. My original drawing of the tank is almost identical to the one I found online today 12-3-22, too. So, I would say this precognition case has a perfect positive correlation.

I wrote a precognition supplement all those years ago, and I had been asking questions like, where is all this leading to? A) Higher activity and proof? B) For outside knowledge and to give proof to others. C) Must know (and come) from <u>within</u> me ... that if there is another reason other than proof ... and proof to <u>me</u> ... why, and what is it?

Victorious troops raise Sri Lankan flag over Jaffna

FROM CHRISTOPHER THOMAS IN COLOMBO

THE Sri Lankan flag was hoisted at noon yesterday in Jaffna City, marking the Government's military victory over the Tamil Tigers in the 12-year civil war and shattering the guerrillas' myth of invincibility.

Up to 50,000 civilians, soldiers, sailors and airmen have died since the war began in July 1983. Hundreds were killed in the latest operation, which took 49 days, to drive the Tigers out of the headquarters of their de facto homeland.

Senior military officers, standing beneath the national flag with its emblem of the lion, spoke of a "great victory" but emphasised that it was over the Tigers, not the 2.5 million Tamil community. The Government is at pains to draw this distinction. It wants Tamils to return to their heartland, and is thus keen to minimise the sense of humiliation and defeat that many feel.

Operation Riviresa (Sunshine) succeeded where others failed because it was backed by unprecedented political and military will. Crucially, India stayed silent, which set the tone for the rest of the international community, despite the displacement of up to 400,000 Tamil civilians.

The Tigers, perceived as fanatical and intransigent, have lost international goodwill. India has spurned them since the 1991 assassination of Rajiv Gandhi, the Prime Minister, allegedly by the Tigers. The fighters now will revert to guerrilla warfare.

The ten Tamil political parties met President Bandaranaike Kumaratunga yesterday to discuss her devolution plans. They want her to press ahead quickly. Sinhalese hardliners, however, will argue that there should be no compromise now the Tigers have been humiliated.

A fresh general election to boost her one-vote majority in the National Assembly may be the only political route left open if she is to retain the trust of the Tamil minority, who have been touched by her admission that many wrongs were committed against them.

The **Battle of Jaffna** was a battle fought from October to December 1995 for the city of Jaffna.[2]

Battle of Jaffna (1995)	
Part of the Sri Lankan civil war	
Date	October 17 - December 5, 1995
Location	Jaffna, Sri Lanka
Result	Sri Lankan Army victory
Belligerents	
Military of Sri Lanka	Liberation Tigers of Tamil Eelam
Commanders and leaders	
Major General **(later General)** Rohan Daluwatte, Brigadier **(later Major General)** Janaka Perera	
Strength	
10,000	Unknown
Casualties and losses	
500 killed (According to Sri Lankan Government claims)[1]	Unknown[1]

Here's a couple of links regarding the conflicts which you may find interesting too.

http://content.time.com/time/world/article/0,8599,1869501,00.html

https://en.m.wikipedia.org/wiki/Battle_of_Jaffna_

PRECOGNITION
SUPPLEMENT

POINTERS

① Precognition activity has shot up
10 fold over last couple of months

Before → getting 1 every 6-8 weeks approx
Now - weekly - (sometimes)!!

② Images in dreams to signify correct
information.
e.g. TAMIL TIGERS
PRECOGNITION

Dec 5/12/95
Bulletin of News
Eve Telegraph.

LOCAL NEWSPAPER

ORANGE BLOBS on
HILL

TOWN of
JAFFNA

JAFFA
ORANGES!!

IN
SRI LANKA

Getting to stage where I am better
at interpreting + also Sports information
is being set so I get the accuracy.
It is their information — accurate but
my perception that gets it wrong sometimes

③ Where is this leading to? ⓐ Higher activity + pro
ⓑ For outside Knowledge
+ to give proof to others ?? (+ come)
ⓒ Must know from within
that if there is another reason either than proof the proof to me
is What + What is it?

Ship(s)/Sea Rescue

Method: Lucid Dream—Tuesday, 25 December 1995.

Time before confirmation/evidence/proof: 1 day—Newspaper reports.

Location/landmarks: SEA.

People: Me watching … one group of people 8/10 (men?)

Day or Night: Night?

Scene: 2 ships close by/next to each other, rescue ships/lifeboats?

Colours: N/A

Smells: N/A

Vehicles: Two large ships side by side.

Feelings: 1 dream last night—precognition?

Dream Log: Tuesday 12-12-95 (bed at 11.05 p.m.) and I awoke 2.40 a.m., and first thoughts was about the timing of such. For some strange reason I thought maybe what occurs between 12am and 4 a.m. indicates the present? And 4 a.m. + the future?? So, as its 2.40 a.m. in the morning = SOON?

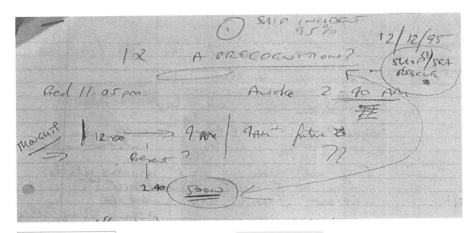

AS IF WATCHING

ONE Group of men??

8/10??

DRAWING

Image of

IF THIS IS PRECOG.
submerged
Bless them all.

This involved the SEA/AT SEA.

Me/ my vision and 'there' too.

2 x Ships? Very large.

Rescue? – Lifeboat over the side.

Going down – pulleys. Into the water.

Image ... so fierce ... of ship speeding into the Sea, as if sloping, almost as if /like a lifeboat down a slope would do.

ALSO, Strong feeling of men sliding about on the deck ... water
SUCH
BAD CONDITIONS

TILTING UP?

Speed slope SHIP
GOING DOWN?
or

DRAWING

AS IF SEA
Coming over it – SUCH FORCE/SPEED

This involved the SEA / AT SEA

Me / my vision + 'thee' too.

2 x Ships ?? — Very large

Rescue ? — life boat over the side
Going down — pulleys into the water.

As if watching

over Group of men ??

[10 ??]

Image no fierce of ship speeding into the sea as if stopping almost as if like sea life boat down a slope would do

Also strong feeling of men sliding around on the deck ??

water SUCH BAD CONDITIONS

Almost square looking

SHIP   SEA

SHIP

LIFE BOATS ??

DARK NIGHT ??

? Image of

TILTING UP

Speed Slope   SHIP GOING DOWN ? OR SUBMERGED ?

AS IF SEA Coming over it

SUCH FORCE + SPEED

If this is such ... them abt.

4 EVENING TELEGRAPH, Wednesday, December 13, 1995

World today

IN BRIEF

Seventeen die in ferry fire

SEVENTEEN people were today feared dead after fire ripped through a ferry off the Philippines.

The blaze spread so quickly that scores of passengers had to jump into the sea without lifejackets.

The fire apparently started in the galley of the MV Kimelody Cristy which was carrying more than 160 passengers and crew.

Navy, coastguard and other passing vessels picked up more than 100 people from the ship which was sailing from Manila to Mindoro island, 78 miles south of the Philippine capital.

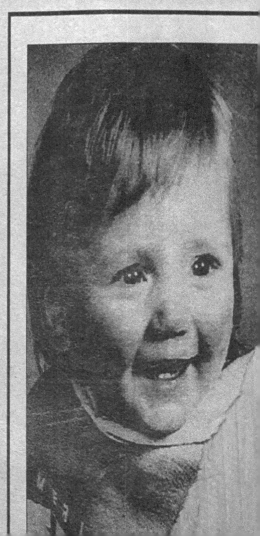

At least 15 dead in ferry fire

MANILA, Philippines (CNN) -- At least 15 people are dead and more than a dozen missing after a ferry caught fire Wednesday off Mindoro Island, south of the Philippine capital.

Survivors and rescuers said the fire aboard the 490-ton Kimelody Cristy spread so rapidly that some people were forced to jump into the sea without lifejackets. Officials estimated there were more than 160 people on board.

Officials said the Coast Guard had three ships scouring the area for more survivors.

The ferry, which could carry more than 400 passengers, was on its way from Manila to Mindoro Island, about 125 kilometers (80 miles) to the south, when the fire broke out in the ferry's galley around 2 a.m.

In 1987, more than 4,000 people died in the world's worst peacetime sea disaster when the ferry Dona Paz collided with a tanker in Philippine waters.

Rear view of the ferry (top).
Another (smaller) rescue boat (below).

Rescue ship alongside the
MV KIMELODY CHRISTY.

Conclusion: (Plus information/dream supplement I'd written). After I woke up my mind became blurry. I was so tired, but I tried to recall/ go over the event seen. Normally I would do these two to three times, sometimes 4 times in my mind ... but this time I fell back asleep!

I reawake (alarm 7.10 a.m.) and immediately tried to think of what I saw ... it was ½ blurry. This could be the realization that I must always remember to keep a pen and paper by the bed—the last time this happened was about one year ago because recall has always been possible and so clear. Maybe I should get a 'torch' pen?

Well, this certainly felt like a precognition after I awoke. The 2 main ships were side by side and looked almost the same as my drawing. (The large rescue ship had the sharp sloping/angled bow and the square looking ship was the ferry). However, there are several anomalies such as the people (group of men) ... were they rescuers or people on the ferry? In addition, had any lifeboats been lowered from the rescue ship?

Within the dream experience, I had no notion of a fire onboard. Apparently, it had started in the ferry's galley at approximately 2.00 a.m. One weird thing is that I awoke at 2.40 a.m., which is exactly when the mayhem/tragedy was occurring. It is almost like I was viewing in real time! My initial thoughts of it being nighttime are therefore accurate, too.

And why were some people sliding around on the deck? Were they simply running about trying to escape? Or, because of the water being sprayed over the ship to help dowse the flames (see earlier picture). Perhaps it also listed at an angle momentarily when the rescue ship sped up to/or alongside it?

And why did I feel the weather/sea was so atrocious? No reports indicted any storm or turbulent sea. Was it simply symbolism for the intensity and chaos and the emotions being so fierce?

So, overall, as there are a lot of similarities in this case with the newspaper report and today's online search (16-3-22), though I'll only give this one moderate correlation. My thoughts and prayers are for those who perished or were injured I what must have been a terrifying ordeal.

There is a link to a YouTube video below, which showed part of the rescue. (**Warning:** There are distressing scenes in this video).

http://www.aparchive.com/metadata/youtube/8a749fc5e6108e4fab68dcffb9f1c860

P.S. I did get a pen with a light ... so I had no excuse in disturbing my better half anymore. It would certainly prove handy for the many precognitions to come—and guess what ... it still works today!

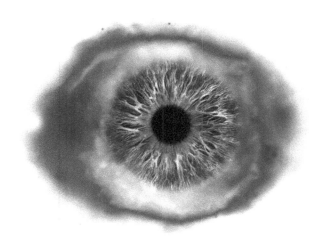

Platform Collapse

Method: Lucid Dreams—Tuesday, 25 December 1995.

Time before confirmation/evidence/proof: 11 years! —Online investigation yielding following reports.

Location/landmarks: Not known.

People: 5 men.

Day or Night: Day

Scene: 5 men working on a platform ... I am watching.

Colours: N/A

Smells: N/A

Vehicles: N/A

Feelings: Danger ... an accident is about to happen. Part collapse and a fall.

Dream Log: It's Christmas night and I go to bed at 11.22 p.m. During my sleep I have nine dreams, of which I felt two (or even three) were precognitions. I awoke at 5.31 a.m., 7.57 a.m. and 9.11 a.m. Perhaps such activity was a spiritual festive gift ... though of course, all very tragic for those involved.

1st dream. There are 5 men working on a platform of some kind. Metal frames—framework. Me ... as if watching. (Strangely, I cannot see anything around the scene ... as if a halo of cloudiness envelopes the outside the platform area itself). There's machinery ... 'cutting' something? I sense danger. The platform—metal (part collapse) and a fall. I witness one man falling. I feel as if a man also survived ... arms damaged, broken? Feeling of hospital? I am viewing as if from the outside ... looking in. Afterwards—some viewing as if 'hospital' ... a man ... in bed ...talking. Saying, "Yeah, lucky, surviving that." I then get fadeout.

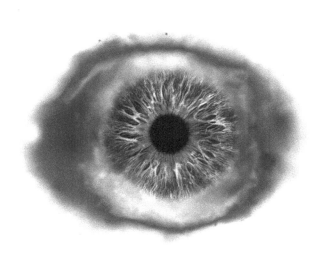

①

1 × 100% CONTAINER
WATER EXPLOSION

XMAS NIGHT 25/12/95

Phew! what a night

Bed
11.22 AM APx

⑨ NINE (/ / / DREAMS)

— 3 Precognition's ?

Yes

A-oke   5-31   AM
             7 57   AM
             9-11   AM.

3 on
12 AM
TODAY

BOXING
DAY
HOURS
.30
-9.30
PM

Brief notes   1ST ↓   ✕ Precog ↘ ? ✕

①   5 MEN   — ME (AS IF watching)   ACCIDENT (cause + affect)
    WORKING   ?

Metal frames - framework   Machinery - cutting
                                  Danger   Man falling
                                  Uinjured   Survived
                                            Arm damaged
                                            Broken ??

cutter ??   Some sort of
              Platform - metal
              (part collapse)

              and a
              fall

Viewing as if from outside   — looking in

Afterwards — same viewing as if in

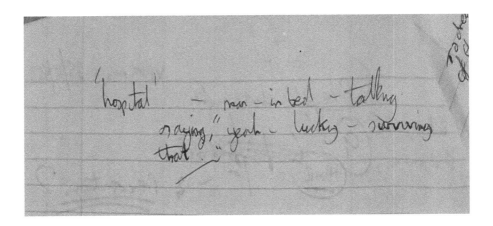

So, I finally found this following 'accident'/tragedy online. This is the first piece of information I had discovered in nearly twenty-seven years ... it dates to 2006! A total of 5 men were on the platform.

⊙ https://www.osha.gov › construction › engineering

Construction Incidents Investigation
Engineering Reports ...

Two construction **workers** fell twenty stories to the ground and died when the stripping **platform** they were working on failed. The incident occurred during the construction of a 22-story condominium building. The **platform** was supported on structural framing resting on the 19th floor concrete slab and on the underside of the 20th floor slab. There were three other employees on the **platform** at the...

Search Investigation Engineering Reports

✚

August 2006: (PDF)

Two construction workers fell twenty stories to the ground and died when the stripping platform they were working on failed. The incident occurred during the construction of a 22-story condominium building. The platform was supported on structural framing resting on the 19th floor concrete slab and on the underside of the 20th floor slab. There were three other employees on the platform at the time of the failure, but they were able to hang onto the railing and the net, and were rescued.

Figure 9

Figure 7

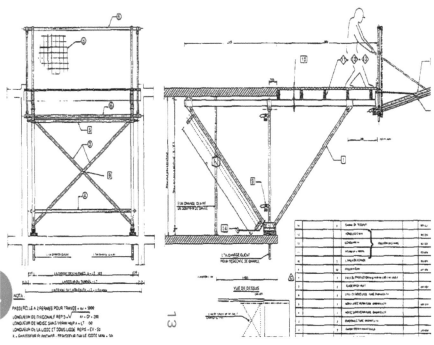

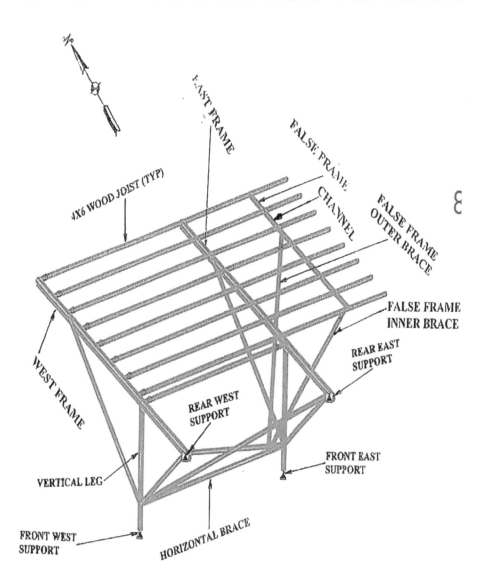

THREE DIMENSIONAL OUTINORD STRIPPING PLATFORM FRAMING

REPORT

On March 1, 2006, at noontime, two construction workers fell twenty stories to the ground and died when the platform they were working on suddenly failed. The platform, known as a "Stripping Platform", was erected about ten days earlier. Platform's purpose was to facilitate rolling out the tunnel forms after concrete was poured on the 21st floor. The platform was supported on structural framing resting on the top of the concrete slab on the 19th floor and on the underside of the 20th floor slab, see figures 1 to 6. There were three other employees on the platform at the time of the failure but they hung onto the railing and the net, and were rescued without any major injuries.

The incident occurred at the construction site of a 22-story condominium building known as "San Marco Place" in downtown Jacksonville, FL. The following were the key participants in the project:

1. The Haskell Company of Jacksonville, FL was the general contractor/ construction manager/Architect.
2. Structural Consultants Associates of Houston, TX was the structural engineer of record.
3. Total Concrete Structures (TCS) was the concrete subcontractor.
4. Skyline Forming (SF) was the subcontractor to TCS.
5. Millennium Forming (MF) was a subcontractor to SF.
6. Outinord Universal (OT) of North Miami Beach, FL was a subcontractor to TCS. Outinord designed and furnished the tunnel forms. OT guided and supervised MF in erecting the tunnel forms and stripping platforms.

Haskell is a design-build company. For this project, they prepared the architectural drawings but the structural design and drawings were outsourced to SCA. Except for the lower floors, Haskell designed the condominium building with parallel walls on each floor spaced generally at about 13' to 19', suitable for tunnel forming. The structural framing of the upper floors consisted of a series of 6" concrete walls instead of conventional dry or CMU walls. The concrete walls ran in two directions, thus providing more than adequate lateral load resistance. The floor to floor height was designed to be 10' high except between the 20th & 21st floors and the 21st & 22nd floors. The floor slabs were typically 6" thick except on the 21st floor where it was 10" thick.

TCS contracted with OT to design and furnish the tunnel forms and stripping platforms. Excluded from the contract were placing, shoring and re-shoring of the concrete slabs. OT was, however, contracted to provide technical assistance and education to TCS's employees to ensure that OT's design was faithfully executed. In case of any deviation from OT's design, OT, though not empowered to stop the work, had enough clout to have the deficiencies corrected immediately.

Tunnel forms consist of pre-fabricated standard steel forms, generally used in pairs to form an inverted L-shape to form a tunnel, and hence the name. When cantilever slabs are to be poured, only one tunnel form as an inverted L-shape is used. The concrete walls and slabs are poured together. The day after the pour, the tunnel forms are ready to be rolled out onto the stripping platform from where a crane lifts them to the next higher floor.

3

Typically, the tunnel forms are 8' in height but higher heights can be attained by add-ons. They come in varying widths, with a maximum of 20'. At the perimeter of the building, stripping platforms are provided to help employees who lubricate the contact surface of the steel forms to prevent them from sticking to the concrete. The tunnel form is rolled out to approximately 45% of its length; employees then attach a lifting triangle to the top of the lifting beam of the tunnel form. The lifting triangle is then fastened to the crane hook. It must be noted that the tunnel forms cantilever approximately 45% of their length, sparing the stripping platform of any dead load of the tunnel forms.

The area of interest where the platform failed was bounded by column lines F.5 to C.9.5 and 1 to 3.5. The platform was known as "Wood Platform 303", as per OT's drawings. The platform consisted of two layers of ¾" plywood supported over 4x6 wood joists spanning in the east-west direction, spaced at about 2'-3" o.c. The wood joists were in turn supported by three steel frames; the east frame, the west frame and the outer false frame. The east and west frames were about 13'- 9" apart. The false frame was approximately 6'-6"east of the east frame. The plywood platform and the 4x6 joists cantilevered about 3'-6" beyond the false frame. The east and west frames were identical and oriented in the north south direction. The north end of the frames were facing the outside of the building. The frames consisted of a horizontal member, equivalent toW6x16, a 3½" round column, and two diagonal braces, on the north and south sides respectively. The exterior and interior braces were 3½"and 3" round pipes, respectively, see figures 1 thru 6. In addition to the main structural members, the east and west frames were braced by round pipes. Each of the east or the west frames was supported at two locations. The bottom of the columns was supported on the top of the 19th floor slab and the top of the interior brace was supported on the underside of the 20th floor slab, see figures 3 thru 5.

The false frame consisted of a horizontal steel channel member equivalent to C 4x7 running in a north-south direction. Unlike the east and west frames, the false frame was not supported by any vertical column. Instead, it was supported by two sloping braces, hereafter called the outside brace and inside brace. Both were approximately 1 7/8" round pipes, see figures 1 thru 7.

As stated earlier, the platform was erected about ten days earlier and had been used on a number of lower floors, beginning from the sixth floor, without any reported problems. In this instance, however, the tunnel forms 16 & 17 extended approximately 8' north of the edge of the slab, though it is highly questionable whether any load from tunnel forms 16 & 17 was imposed on the platform. There was another difference which arose from the fact that the clear floor height between the 21st floor and the 20th floor was 10'-2" instead of the usual 9'-6". Due to the increased height, the contractor placed three 2x12 to make up the difference in height. Our analysis indicates that the cribbings had little impact on the incident. Therefore, the platform was essentially used in the same manner as it was on the lower floors. In our analysis, we have discounted any load from the tunnel forms on the platform.

There were five employees on the platform at the time of the incident. The tunnel forms No. 16 and 17 were in place and were being leveled. Concrete was not placed over the forms. The forms protruded about 8 feet beyond the edge of the slab. As stated earlier, the forms were practically imposing no load on the platform. The failure occurred under the dead load plus the loads of the five employees.

The failure resulted in the platform tilting downward at the northeast corner. The column of the east frame buckled making a right angle at about 1'-8" above the base. The exterior and interior braces of the east frame bowed approximately 2" and 4", respectively. Most significantly the outside brace of the false frame buckled about 15". The inside brace of the false frame also buckled approximately 5½". Other bracing members also were distressed, see Figures 7 thru 18.

Structural Analysis:

The purpose of the structural analysis was to determine whether the platform framing was appropriately designed to support the loads imposed on it on the day of the incident and whether the design was based upon a factor of safety of four, as required by OSHA standards. The factor of safety is required under live loads only. The following assumptions were made:

1. Tunnel forms No. 16 and 17 did not impose any load on the platform.
2. A load factor of 1.0 was used. No capacity reduction was employed.
3. The critical buckling load of the exterior brace of the false frame was computed on the classic Euler's formula and as per LRFD provisions of AISC specifications.
4. The weight of the five people was assumed to be 200 pounds each plus 50 pounds each for the equipment was added, as per industry practice. Analysis was also done assuming the weight of the employees to be 150 pounds plus 50 pounds for the equipment.
5. The five workers were placed at different locations at the north east end of the platform to determine the stresses.
6. Only gravity load was considered. Wind was disregarded.
7. The yield strength of the exterior brace of the false frame was considered to be 35,000 psi.

Commercially available STAAD.Pro. 2005 was used to model the platform and its framing. A number of analyses were done to determine the impact of the live loads on the structural integrity of the platform. The column supports on the concrete slab were modeled as pinned connections and so were the supports of the frame at the underside of the floor slab above.

First only dead load was considered. The dead load was computed to be approximately 4,460 pounds, including the dead load of the two layers of plywood, eight 4x6 joists, the east and west frames, the false frames and all the bracings. Under these conditions, the platform was not distressed. See table I for the magnitude of the vertical reactions.

Second, in addition to the dead load, five workers each weighing 250 pounds, including their equipment loads, were considered. The five workers were placed on the top of the false frame channel at the spacing of the wood joists. The first worker was placed at the junction of the most exterior 4x6 joist and the false frame channel. The assumption that all four supports were pinned proved to be inaccurate and, therefore, the pinned support of the rear west frame was removed. The outside brace of the false frame was subjected to an axial compressive force of 1,065 pounds. The force on the outside brace did not vary, regardless of the assumed end conditions of the outside brace, i.e., whether pinned or fixed.

Third, in addition to the dead load, five workers were placed at the extreme edge of the platform parallel to the east side, spaced at 2'-3" o.c. beginning from the northeast corner. Again, the workers were spaced over the location of the 4x6 joists. The axial force in the false frame's outside brace then jumped to 2,150 pounds.

Fourth, in addition to the dead load, three employees were placed over the most exterior north joist, evenly spaced over the 3'-6" cantilever, and two employees were placed over the next exterior joist over the cantilever. The force in the outer brace was computed to be 2,400 pounds. When the weight of the employees was reduced to 200 pounds inclusive of the equipment weight, the force was reduced to 1,920 pounds, still greater than the failure load.

Fifth, in addition to the dead load, only three workers were considered. They were placed at the outer edge of the platform parallel to the east side, beginning from the northeast corner. They were spaced over the top of the 4x6 joists. The outer brace axial strength was reduced to 1,550 pounds.

All the above analyses did not consider the increased live load to account for the factor of safety as required by OSHA. The analyses were conducted based on the actual loads. Intuitively, the structural framing looked precarious because of the lack of any vertical support of the false frame. The false frame was supported on two inclined braces, with the outer brace being approximately 16' long. The analyses confirmed that the outer brace of the false frame was the most critical member. The brace was sized to be approximately 1.9" round pipe with a wall thickness of approximately 1/8". The analysis indicated that the platform framing was highly sensitive to the location and number of workers on the platform. The farther the employees were located in the northeast corner of the platform, the higher was the axial force in the outer brace of the false frame. It is likely that the employees were closer to each other than was assumed in the analysis, which could further increase the axial load.

The buckling load of the outer brace was computed to be 2,174 pounds as per Euler's formula and 1890 pounds as per LRFD provisions of AISC. Euler's formula is derived under ideal conditions, therefore, LRFD formula is more reliable and is the industry standard. Under the loading pattern of the fourth analysis, discussed above, the axial force in the outside brace of the false frame was computed to be 2,400 and 1,920 pounds under the weights of employees of 250 and 200 pounds respectively, inclusive of equipment weights of 50 pounds. The weights did not include any factors of safety.

The same platform was used a number of times from the sixth floor and above without any reported problem. Lack of earlier failures could be attributed to less than five employees on the platform or employees at locations away from the northeast corner of the platform. From the very beginning, the platform was in a precarious structural state even though no failure had previously occurred.

<u>Conclusions:</u>

1. Outinord's structural design was flawed in that the false frame was not appropriately supported and the outer brace was not correctly proportioned. When the live loads of five employees, without any factor of safety, were placed near the northeast corner of the platform, failure became imminent.

2. Outinord's structural design did not incorporate the required factor of safety of four under live load. OSHA standard 1926.451(a) (1) was violated.

3. Outinord's structural design was not performed as per the industry standard.

4. Wind was not a contributing factor.

Conclusion: The investigation of the 1 MARCH 2006 Collapse of the Stripping Platform at San Marco Place, Jacksonville, FL USA was carried out by the U.CS Department of Labor, occupational Safety and Health in August that year. I have highlighted several interesting sentences which help to correlate the original drawing and dream log.

As I mentioned, the bizarre thing with the first dream is the period before I'd find any sort of evidence/proof and the 'event' being actualized. Most precognitions have been a day, a few days, or several weeks, but no longer than that. How and why, this occurred, I do not know.

In addition, even with many years' notice, there's no way I could try to warn anyone in such circumstances ... which demonstrates that as human beings we do not yet have the ability and power to intervene—without the precise location and time. But do we even have the right to do so? Surely, such things are under God's control? And we know in truth, we cannot live or impact another's karma, either. So, when you consider point one in the safety report's conclusion above (which states that the platform failure became imminent) ... are these so-called 'accidents' simply cause and effect?

Overall, I feel the flat shape of the platform and the downward poles I drew—looks very much like the one in the photographs—with the 5 men working on it. In addition, viewing one man falling and then watching one of the men who survived in hospital, I believe this case has a perfect positive correlation. I only hope they enhanced safety protocols to prevent this sort of an unfortunate event from ever happening again. May those construction workers RIP.

Boiler Explosion

Method: Lucid Dreams—Tuesday, 25 December 1995 continued.

Time before confirmation/evidence/proof: 3 days—Newspaper report 28 December 1995 and a short online article found in 2022.

Location/landmarks: Room/building.

People: One person (man?).

Day or Night: Night.

Scene: Someone walking by a container (water) of some sorts.

Colours: N/A

Smells: N/A

Vehicles: N/A

Feelings: Danger/concerns over a container about to explode—sense of precognition.

Dream Log: This was dream five of nine on Christmas night. Me travelling—in a car—driving. Seems familiar 'scenery'—roads—roundabout. Drive around + over it—to a house. Me sitting with Caroline—but Caroline from work? Felt that way? But 'Blurred' for a second. Then, watching TV or felt as if me being 'there'. Something—danger water explosion 'contained' water of some kind.

Something is wrong. Then, as if outside looking in ... watching someone/something holding a container? If it explodes there's danger ...

'boiling' water will burn/blister them (?) Who? It's like I'm trying to say 'think' to whoever ... be careful—be careful!!!

Thought a hot water bottle??/container (see drawing) Precog or Explosion of emotions to bursting point. Single person. Boiler-water container. Blast.

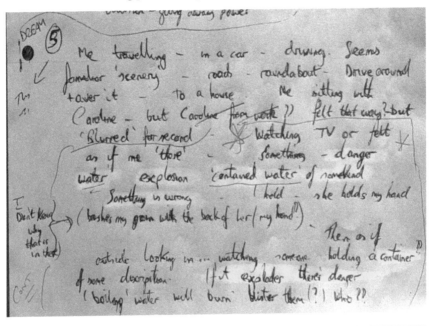

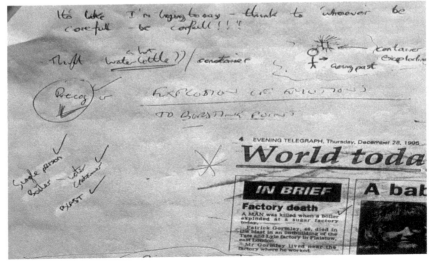

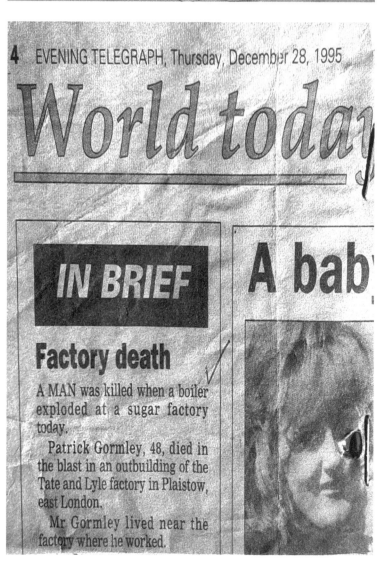

...g to say – think to 'whoever' be
...orful ! ! ?

) / container   S.   _container_
Exploding
going past

4 EVENING TELEGRAPH, Thursday, December 28, 1995

World today

IN BRIEF

A bab

Factory death

A MAN was killed when a boiler exploded at a sugar factory today.

Patrick Gormley, 48, died in the blast in an outbuilding of the Tate and Lyle factory in Plaistow, east London.

Mr Gormley lived near the factory where he worked.

Re: Tate and Lyle sugar factory in london accident / death in 1995

« Reply #2 on: Yesterday at 20:59 »

Aberdeen Press & Journal 29 Dec 1995

"A worker was killed when an explosion tore through an outbuilding at a Tate & Lyle sugar factory in Plaistow, London, early yesterday. Patrick Gormley (48) of Silvertown, East London, died from his injuries after the boiler exploded."

Reading Evening Post 28 Dec 1995

adds ... *"of Boxley St, Silvertown ... explosion at 1.15am"*

Here is some some interesting information regarding 'Tate and Lyle.'

Sugar refining

Former Tate & Lyle PLC refinery along the
Thames in Silvertown, London

The company was formed in 1921 from a merger of two rival sugar refiners: *Henry Tate & Sons* and *Abram Lyle & Sons*.[3]

Henry Tate established his business in 1859 in Liverpool, later expanding to Silvertown in East London.[3] He used his industrial fortune to found the Tate Institute in Silvertown in 1887 and the Tate Gallery in Pimlico, Central London in 1897. He endowed the gallery with his own collection of Pre-Raphaelite paintings.[4]

Abram Lyle, a cooper and shipowner, acquired an interest in a sugar refinery in 1865 in Greenock and then at Plaistow Wharf, West Silvertown, London.[3] The two companies had large factories nearby each other – Henry Tate in Silvertown and Abram Lyle at Plaistow Wharf – so prompting the merger. Prior to the merger, which occurred after they had died, the two men were bitter business rivals, although they had never met in person.[5] In 1949, the company introduced its "Mr Cube" brand, as part of a marketing campaign to help it fight a proposed nationalisation by the Labour government.[3]

Diversification ✎

From 1973, British membership of the European Economic Community threatened Tate & Lyle's core business, with quotas imposed from Brussels favouring domestic sugar beet producers over imported cane refiners such as Tate & Lyle.[6] As a result, under the leadership of Saxon Tate (a direct descendant of Henry Tate), the company began to diversify into related fields of commodity trading, transport and engineering, and in 1976, it acquired competing cane sugar refiner Manbré & Garton.[6]

In 1976, the Company acquired a 33% stake (increased to 63% in 1988) in *Amylum*, a European starch-based manufacturing business.[3] The

The following images represent this iconic brand perfectly. This is a real favourite of mine btw ... poured over sponge puddings and the British classic, 'spotted dick'. Awesomeness personified ... and if you haven't tried it, you're missing out big time! Here is a YouTube video if you ever fancy making it. Enjoy.

https://youtu.be/fu15XOF-ros

TATE & LYLE

1883

Abram Lyle & Sons opened Plaistow Refinery in London

Abram Lyle & Sons started melting sugar at Plaistow Refinery, only a short distance from Henry Tate & Son's Thames Refinery. Lyle's Golden Syrup was an instant hit and Lyle was soon selling a tonne a week.

Find out more about Abram Lyle >

TATE & LYLE

1885

Lyle's Golden Syrup first filled into tins

These iconic green and gold tins feature the world's oldest branding. Originally made in small quantities and sold in wooden casks to employees and locals, as demand grew, casks were swapped for large dispensers found on the shelves of grocery stores. Today, more than a million of these same tins leave Plaistow each month.

TATE ⬟ LYLE

Type	Public limited company
Traded as	LSE: TATE ⬏
	FTSE 250 **component**
Industry	Food processing
Founded	**Merger of** Henry Tate & Sons **(established 1859) and Abram Lyle & Sons (established 1887) in 1921**
Headquarters	London, England, UK
Key people	Gerry Murphy, Chairman
	Nick Hampton, CEO
Products	Starches
	Splenda
	Alcohol
	Citric acid
	High fructose corn syrup
Revenue	▼ £2.807 billion (2021)[1]
Operating income	▼ £287 million (2021)[1]
Net income	▲ £253 million (2021)[1]
Number of employees	4,400 (2021)[1]
Website	www.tateandlyle.com ⬏

Re: accident at tate and lyle

« **Reply #4 on:** Wednesday 07 September 11 12:50 BST (UK) »

Silvertown apparently was notorious for accidents, (it looks as if it still is) and explosions in particular, as it was the centre of the chemical industry. I have an ancestor who was killed in an explosion at a chemical works called Bolton and Birts in 1880.

Conclusion: Yet another fatality ... R.I.P Mr. Gormley. The short note above came from a kind soul after I queried the incident on RootsChat. com ... a very helpful site. I had also emailed Tate and Lyle via their website but have heard nothing back. Maybe they don't want to drag up the past? And if there was company negligence (regarding faulty equipment), perhaps they just didn't want any further publicity? It would be of interest to establish the cause of the blast though.

I believe this is another case with perfect positive correlation. My dream only involved a single person. The container/explosion was accurate. It showed the event took place during the night ... and it occurred at 1:15 a.m. It is sad that my simple attempt at warning of the danger was to no avail. Will it ever be possible to transcend the dream world—with thoughts and/or sound—in real 'time'?

I remember a verse in a poem entitled 'Spirit and Soul', that I channeled many years ago. It's in my previous book entitled, Rhyme and Reason— Spiritual Poetry and Prose to Strengthen Your Heart, Uplift Your Soul, and Define Your Purpose, which seems to fit here.

Your tears of love that fall and do shine,
Contain the light that is yours ... and also of mine.
While certain events happen and they cannot be changed,
The karmic slate to wipe clean and must be forever erased.

There were other dreams that night and one involved 2 men breaking out from a prison. They had detonators and had been waiting for some electrical current to pass through (or by) which would trigger a blast, strong enough to create a small hole in a wall. I spent a few hours online trying to discover this event without success. Perhaps this has an even longer timescale to a precognitive event ... I'll let you know!

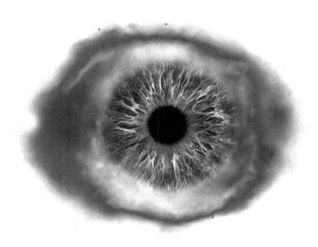

Epilogue

I must have received hundreds—if not thousands—of dreams over the years; this book concentrates on precognitions in my journals of 1994 and 1995. My next book will focus on those from 1996 and 1997, with a few recent ones too. Among them are 'accidents' such as a helicopter crash and a sea rescue, but there are some light-hearted ones too. Thankfully, they are not all about death or destruction!

It's no surprise that in the lines above, I'm clearly thinking ahead. But why is it that social media, television, business gurus, life coaches (and even our relatives) deem it so important to do this? These questions always come to the fore: 'Where would you like to be next year? Or, in five or ten years' time?' Mm … let us all hail the mantra, 'If you don't plan, you are planning to fail.'

What about spontaneity and adventure, living in the moment, or taking one day at a time?

As you progress through the material world, this natural interest in what the future holds (or at least in what a present situation is trying to tell you in your life) appears to transfix your gaze … like cat's-eyes captured by moonlight. Yet this is where your thoughts may become limited. They will often reflect negatively upon work, career, financial matters, your mental and physical health, and your relationships, too.

Please also understand, the innate desire to control every aspect of one's daily existence only occurs because the mind wishes to dictate. It attempts to project imaginary future outcomes based purely upon your experiences. You, accordingly, make emotional decisions through fear and dread of loss, rather than for joy and peace and bliss. Perhaps this is why many people believe forms of 'fortune telling' are external 'props' used as a crux!

In addition, curiosity seems to be rising surrounding time travel and how this might affect all our 'yesterdays'. The idea of breaking through the linear barrier of time and travelling to any point in history is fascinating. In theory, if you travel faster than the speed of light (which is 186,282 miles per second), then it may become workable. But throw gravity, matter, anti-matter into the equation and wonder, could we really prevent accidents, tragedies, and catastrophes that transpire around the world?

If you are a fan of Marvel's Avengers, here's a reminder of how the Hulk defines this quandary in the brilliant film, *Endgame*: 'If you travel to the past, the past becomes your future and your former present becomes your past, which can't now be changed by your new future.'

Er ... sort of makes sense!

What's more frightening is that, one day, mankind might be so preoccupied with trying to fix everything ... they'll never stop to think whether they should. Would our interference have greater consequences that are perhaps even disturbing some divine plan for us all?

Such is the changeable quality of the 'future' that clarity may only occur with careful and cautious study through contemplation of our dreams and their symbols, and of those images and messages revealed within the vast array of divination methods too. And should you pursue this route, feasibly, with practice, you could then make effective choices in your life, which may influence your destiny. That said, any ability (or lack of) could also be karmic, but you can still expand your knowledge, allowing you to serve your 'fellow man' with selfless love in the process.

Trusting God is the only real alternative. Of course. Understandably, the starving, those who live in poverty, or have ill health might find this very difficult to do. However, through faith and hope, please realise that we are all stronger than we could ever imagine.

Regardless of where you put your trust, a soul needs to connect with their own divinity and go beyond the boundary of their senses. We achieve this through our heart's centre, where our love and power reside and resonate inside.

And who is to say we aren't meant to discover our spiritual and psychic gifts along the way? After all, they may have been instilled within us—pre-sent since the dawn of awakening.

Perhaps this book will inspire your own development and encourage you to take full responsibility for your future. And, if you are just starting your inner journey of discovery (or simply find this a difficult concept to grasp), then I hope the following glossary—which also contains spiritual references—can help you determine a suitable method to learn and practise, allowing it to guide you forward to know your own truth.

No matter what form of divination you pursue and utilise, whether that's rune stones, cards, candle wax, mirrors, or indeed any object, even a flower, I believe we are all tapping into the universal energy that flows through everything.

Therefore, what is holding you back?

Start unleashing the power of your psychic gifts to predict the future … today!

P.S. To anyone connected to the people in my precognitions, please know my heart is with you. Remember, the divine, Source, God shall always be your guide and confidante as you continue your earth-plane sojourn.

Love and light to one and all,
David.

A Divination and Spiritual Reference Guide

Abundance: Awaken your consciousness, to the knowingness of your own creative abundant energy, a part of creation.

Affirmations: Help us to purify our thoughts and restructure the dynamic of our brains. Personal affirmations are positive, specific sentences which need to be in the present tense, often repeated several times to encourage or motivate yourself. The word affirmation comes from Latin 'affimare', originally meaning "to make steady, strengthen."

Amen: A Hebrew word that means "so be it". Usually said at the end of a prayer, we are asking God, "Please let it be as we have prayed". NB. When people place their hands/palms together it signifies a negative and positive flow of energy. The left receives and the right sends. The same hand gesture is a customary Hindu and Buddhist greeting called Namaste but is also used when leave-taking too. It is sometimes spoken as Namaskar or Namaskaram.

Angel: The word "angel" is derived from the Greek word angelos which means 'messenger'. They are divine spirits, each of God's consciousness and these beings of light intercede for us, answering our prayers and calls for help. In Hinduism, they are called devas or devis. In Islam, a belief in

Angels who materialise out of light and function as Allah's messengers is one of the six pillars of faith.

Archangel: Hierarchs (leaders) of the Angels.

Ascension: Is the process whereby the soul, (having balanced /removed karma and fulfilled its divine plan) merges first with the universal/Christ consciousness and then with the living presence of the I AM THAT I AM. Once the Ascension has taken place, the soul becomes a permanent atom of the 'Body of God'. Please remember, your ascension is not something you plan for or takes place on a certain date. You are actively choosing a process to evolve into higher consciousness ... through expanded awareness and integrating the higher reverberation of your spiritual self. So, the act of ascending; is to climb to a greater plane/dimension which involves total transformation on all levels (all that you are) ... realigned with divine love. In Christian belief, the ascent of Jesus Christ into Heaven on the 40th day after his resurrection ... his return to sit on the right-hand side of the 'Father'.

Assumptions: You must remove all assumptions. Children are getting 'raised' and many of their parent's beliefs are being superimposed upon them. But how can anyone perceive 'God'/Creator/life-energy when they do not even understand the full nature of 'existence'? Do not assume anything ... you only need to experience it.

Astral Projection: A breaking free by the astral 'body', believed to occur just before death or during some dreams. Also known as out-of-body experience (OBE).

Atma: The soul, universal consciousness.

Aum: This is the universal, sacred, and indestructible sound. The frequency of the same word that went forth as the origin of creation ... the basis and root of all sounds of your existence. By sounding the AUM comes our oneness and can provide many benefits to the body and mind. It is a spiritual process unaffected by culture or language and is the pathway to how your energies function. Each letter stands for a component of our divinity and is intended to be sounded separately ... with repetition and great awareness as the reverberation flows within you, moving from the navel to the tip of your nose. (Remember to pronounce the letters as Aa's, Ooo's and Mmm's). The A comes forth from Alpha (our Father) as the initiator, the creator, the beginning of consciousness of being ... the thrust of power. The M is the is the OM (our Mother) the conclusion/ending... one with the Holy Spirit–therefore the positive and negative polarities of being are pronounced. From the A to the Om, all the vastness of creation is contained and so the U in the centre is the cup cradling you (the centre piece)—the real self in universal manifestation—so, A-U-M is the Trinity in unity. In the East, Hindus refer to the Trinity as Brahma, Vishnu, and Shiva ... the relevant forces of Creation, Maintenance and Destruction. In the West... the Trinity is Father, Son, and the Holy Spirit. NB. The meaning in Sanskrit is "I bow, I agree, I accept". I bow before God Almighty, I agree that I am the 'son', and I accept my immortal destiny.

Aura: An invisible emanation or field of energy believed to radiate from a person or object.

Auric Field: Your chakra system, subtle bodies and other subtle energy points create an interconnecting field of energy around the physical body.

Automatic writing: A type of divination where the pen appears to direct the writer instead of the writer directing the pen. In a paranormal sense, automatic writing is synonymous with autography, psychography and spirit writing. Some who experience this phenomenon have also written in other languages which they do not even speak! So, with pen in hand, the writer basically sits back, clears his mind, and waits for the pen, which appears to take on a life of its own. Although autography—meaning in one's own handwriting—is the least accurate synonym for automatic writing. In addition, spiritualists believe that automatic writing is a form of spirit 'contact' with the living; hence the name 'spirit writing'. Others also believe that automatic writing is the elimination of mental censorship and the ability to tap the thoughts of the unconscious mind (psychography).

Awareness: Is vital to your progress as a seeker to connect with your divine nature. Therefore, you must become aware of the external chatter which detracts from your inner enquiry. Do not just 'observe' but give your full attention to your consciousness—not the body and mind. And it will help if you only focus on one activity at a time … so do not multitask. This way, divinity will manifest through you! Remember, the less you do, the less personality is involved and the more 'aware' of life you become.

Axinomancy: This is divination by throwing an axe or hatchet and observing the direction of the handle or (sometimes with a saw) then interpreting the quivering of the blade! Bizarre to say the least!

Balance: We know that karma is action, and all your experiences of joy, misery, happiness, and suffering happen within you. Once you have truly grasped the fact that this encompasses your entire system of mind, body, soul, and energy, it can be the springboard to finding true balance. This becomes easier if you don't let the mind work against you … a necessity to experience the divinity and bring brilliance into your life. So, try to attain this through every aspect your physicality, your diet, thoughts, sleep, posture and breathing … everything!

Belomancy: Divination by shooting, tossing, or balancing an arrow.

Bliss/blissful: This is not a goal or attainment in itself. You need to make it your purpose, the foundation and way of your life. Everything else plays out from this.

Body: The vessel (some call it a shell, overcoat, or even a bubble) which houses our senses through which we perceive everything. The physical body is also shaped by our evolutionary and genetic memory. It thrives or withers by the food we eat, inherited from Mother Earth, and nourished by creation. In addition, it allows the faith and goodwill of the divine intent.

Bondage: What we have created for ourselves materialises from nothing more than our likes and dislikes. Bondage also refers to the identification we have placed upon our bodies and minds, and not with people, places, or material/physical objects. It all lies in your mind ... your thoughts. One who considers themselves free becomes free. One who considers themselves bound remains bound. So, you are what you think and therefore if you think you are just body and mind you are ... if you think you are boundless you are! Ironically, use your thoughts to go beyond the bondage of your thoughts! Remember, there is no bondage in consciousness.

Brontoscopy: Interpreting the sound of thunder.

Burning: Divination through the sacrifice of children by burning! Apparently, the Phoenicians and Carthaginians sacrificed their children to Kronos as a mode of obtaining an oracle during times of grave national danger or calamity.

Carromancy: Divination by observing melting wax.

Causal body: The highest and innermost 'body' which veils the Atma/soul. A doorway to higher consciousness.

Chakras: The Chakra 'system' is a vital part of our mental, emotional, physical, and spiritual 'bodies'. There are 112 funnel-shaped energy points within... and 2 'outside' of us.

Chiromancy: Divination through the study of the hand, fingers, fingernails, and palms.

Clairaudience: Claire means "clear" in French and means clear 'hearing'. It is the psychic ability to hear voices, sounds, and messages from beyond the physical world. Psychics who are clairaudient hear voices, sounds or music that are not audible to the normal ear. They receive these messages mentally or within their ears. Possessing this skill may provide you with a clear path of communication between yourself and higher spirits or beings.

Claircognizance: means clear 'knowing'. It's a metaphysical sense where you know something to be correct but may be unable to back up your statement with fact or how you came into that information. People with this psychic gift are often quite logical and tend to receive psychic information through spontaneous ideas. Claircognizants also enjoy processing through a problem to find creative solutions. They have an inner knowing or gut feeling that they can't dismiss ... even if they try.

Clairsentience: Being sentient is the ability to perceive or feel things, hence clear-feeling ... defined as "having the ability to perceive things clearly." One senses subtle energies around them, and feel the emotional state of things, such as the emotions in a room, possibly from a person or an object. To be clairsentient you will probably be highly sensitive and emphatic. whereby your heart and energy body tune into the energy around you, so that it can be perceived, felt, and understood.

Clairvoyance: It comes from two French words "clair" and "voyance", meaning "clear vision" or clear-sightedness. This ability connects you with your intuition via visions, images, and symbols. For some people, possessing a clairvoyant ability and psychic seeing are as natural as breathing. However, for others, their intuitive gifts are present and undeniable ... but need consistent psychic development to flourish. It can also be deemed as a form of extrasensory perception (ESP). Spiritualists also use the term to mean seeing or hearing the spirits of the dead that are said to surround the living.

Cleromancy: Dice divination is a simple tool that helps you find solutions to your day-to-day problems. In fact, dice and dominoes have been used as a diving method since ancient times.

Compassion: A frequency of divine love coming from the soul through the heart chakra.

Consciousness: Intellect without memory ... pure and unsullied by the mind's impressions and body experiences.

Cyclomancy: Divination through interpreting the revolutions of a spinning bottle or top, or even a turning wheel.

Death: The important aspect here is that you must experience to 'know'. Therefore, one has to acknowledge what you do or do not know, and what you believe or disbelieve too. Death is fiction, death is life, death is a continuation. When the body dies it has become unsustainable for life (your soul), so the conscious mind moves on, retaining all qualities bar discrimination. We need to relate this to karma yet again, for it acts like a bubble retaining the soul within the body. Imagine the bubble has burst and the air within now merges with totality, and so becomes enlightened.

Decrees: Relate to the science of the spoken word. A step up from all prayer forms both East and West, they combine prayer, meditation, and visualisation, and place a special emphasis on affirmations using the name of God—I AM THAT I AM. An effective method in balancing karma, spiritual resolution, and soul advancement.

Destiny: People often blame a negative outcome as a result of their so-called destiny, but in doing so they place a total limitation upon their life and so cannot be free. However, it is you (and only you) who makes your life! We could also define destiny as what you create for yourself.

Determinism (in the universe versus 'randomness'): Occurrences in nature are causely decided by proceeding events or natural laws … that everything leading up to this point has happened for a reason. Everything has a purpose and is determined. (Some people state that free will is therefore an illusion, that internal and external forces govern our behaviour, of which we have no control). In contrast, the theory of randomness is that it is all just coincidence! The fact that we even exist is nothing but a result of a complex, inevitable string of chemical accidents and biological mutations. There is no grand meaning and there is no 'purpose'. This is an interesting debate … what do you think?

Déjà vu: is actually a French term, which directly means 'already seen' or 'already dreamt.' Technically speaking, one experiences this through our visual perception rather than our senses. It is our eyes that notice that a particular event has repeated itself. Have you ever seen the film Matrix ... where Neo sees the same black cat twice? It is like witnessing time rewind right before your eyes, with a brisk, stunning sensation of having already lived a totally identical situation in some undefined past. The feeling that you've done this exact same thing once before—been in this place, engaged in this conversation, had the same 'feeling'—which suddenly overwhelms you. You might get goose-bumps. N.B. One of the earliest explanations of déjà vu was St. Augustine's in the fifth century ... "The person has the impression that he is reliving an experience he has had previously while asleep."

Devotion: All forms of devotion arise from your emotions. It provides you with a sense of freedom and comes from the heart... unlike belief, which materialises from the mind. It is what is devoid of 'you' ... and allows grace to flow through you. One may experience this by allowing a greater intelligence to work through you whilst keeping your intellect at bay.

Divinity: The state or quality of being divine.

Divination: The word divination comes from the Latin word *divinare*, meaning 'to foresee' or 'to be inspired by a God'. The act of obtaining secret knowledge, especially that which relates to the future. In essence there are two main species ... artificial and inspirational ... or, as it was called in ancient times—natural divination. Artificial divination depends on the skill of the person in reading and interpreting certain signs called omens. In inspirational or natural divination, the diviner is supposedly under the immediate influence of some spirit or God who enables them to see the future. Throughout history, people have always sought ways to predict their future and guide them along the 'correct' path ... to obtain insight into a question or situation by way of an occultic, standardized process, or ritual. Therefore, to engage in forms of divination is to reveal mysterious knowledge by 'supernatural' practices. It is also correlated with the occult and often involves fortune-telling or soothsaying, as it used to be called. Used in various forms, diviners ascertain their interpretations of how a querent should proceed ... by reading the signs/omens, or through alleged contact with a supernatural agency. There are dozens—and possibly hundreds—of methods of prediction (which fit into the category of divination) that you may choose to use in your 'magical' practice. Some people try many different things, but you may find that you are more gifted in one method than another. If you decide to pursue different types of divination methods, see which works best for you and your abilities. Remember, 'Spirit' always says not to force such things, and it better to allow them to unfold naturally. One may strive to achieve, but practice does not necessarily make perfect.

Dowsing or Divining: Sometimes refeed to as 'water witching' ... using a rod (or two rods) to determine the location of water.

Dreams: The actual name for divination by dream interpretation is called 'Oneiromancy'. This is a massive area for debate and would take many pages (and books) to do the subject justice. So, we'll only be taking a short glimpse, a snapshot if you like into the secret language of sleep. Dreams are a flow of thoughts, images, and sensations that happen in the mind when we are asleep. Psychologists are divided over the function and meaning of dreaming. Sigmund Freud believed they are a 'window' into our unconscious mind ... and represent our memories, feelings, and emotions that we try to suppress during our waking hours. Therefore, dreams ease repression by allowing these memories to be reinstated. In ancient history, people had believed their dreams were messages from the 'God's. In this present era, some think they're no more than a reflection/an expression of the previous day's activities (a digestion process in which these issues are worked through) ... or just because they've eaten too much cheese! But what really causes them? Is it your soul sending sublime hints and clues to help you in your life? Are they from a non-visible awareness (your psyche), where you can reach out to for guidance? And why are there so many types of dreams? In one you could be the observer, in another you're the participant. Or its vicarious, whereby you feel you are experiencing events—as if in another's skin. It might also be symbolic, where a home could mean security or comfort to one person but a source of anxiety/criticism to another. How about a shared dream ... as if a telepathic link connects you to a friend or relative? Then there's psychic dreams, like the precognitions within this book. One thing's for sure though, in every dream ... the crucial element is always you! In addition, there's 'Lucid' dreams in which you realize in the dream that you are dreaming, providing the opportunity to influence the dream itself. When you ask a question within it you may get a response. These offer possibilities to help you grow and understand yourself (and others) ... opening doors for latent talents or even self-healing. In time, you may be able to bring this lucid state into your wakened reality, to become more spontaneous in life. (Always try to be positive and selfless within these types of dreams.) An important aspect is you are relating to inner wisdom. Try to value this relationship, respect it. Become more fulfilled by exploring consciously your unconscious mind ... to break through and transcend time and space. So, let's also be clear ... everybody dreams. Some say they don't, but they do. They are likely to occur during REM sleep, which accounts for about 20-25 of our total sleep 'time'. In fact, research shows that we all dream about 2 hours per night, with each dream lasting from about 5 up to 20 mins! Interestingly, about 95% of dreams are forgotten by the time you get out of bed. But perhaps it's the degree of importance (held by the dreamer) whether they're actually recalled or not? However, don't fret if you want to remember them but can't. One helpful tip is to have a dream diary/journal/writing pad to record your dreams. By having a form of record by your side you will impress upon mind the desire to dream, and you will start to recall them more often. You could simply make your dream diary/log notes on the left of the page and your thoughts/interpretations on the right. One tip is to make a brief note of anything important that happened during the preceding day and what was also coming up the following day too. This gives you a 'reference' point to work from should you need to interpret it at a later date. In analysing your dreams, you can learn about your deep secrets and hidden feelings. Remember that no one is a better expert at interpreting them than yourself. This is because each dreamer has their own dream "language". Dream dictionaries may give an overview, but dream elements will be unique to your own interpretation. You can do this by asking it questions such as:

- What am I doing in the dream?
- Does the dream want anything from me?
- How am I acting within it?
- What/who is the adversary/or providing help?
- Am I trying to avoid anything?
- Is it suggesting that you need to act in some way?
- What are the major symbols, issues, conflicts, relationships within it?
- How am I feeling in the dream?

Remember, before you start to analysis your dream, try to become 'still', perhaps with meditation or through breathing techniques. When you quieten the mind and body, it's more likely that you will become receptive and open to what the dream is trying to tell you. Whatever opinion you have regarding dreams, know they can often prepare us for our life tasks and journey ahead.

Earth-plane: The world of material form.

East and West: East is often related to the destruction of all that is unreal… and the purification of the veil of Maya (illusion) by Lord Shiva. West is usually termed with the action of the Holy Spirit.

Ego: The ego is the unconscious/lower self, and it only identifies with the body and mind. However, in truth this lower self does not really exist … it is only an absence of awareness, just like darkness which is the absence of light. So, one cannot be aware of and also ecstatic/blissful at the same time. In contrast, your reality is the infinite or higher self ... pure intelligence. Remember, you do not need to 'see' to identify with the 'all knowing' ... and when you remove the ego you are able to experience pure joy.

Enlightenment: Everything is lit up; you see the reality of life/existence. True insight and comprehension.

ESP: Extra sensory literally means "outside the senses". ESP is the ability to receive and process information independent of our five senses of sight, touch, hearing, smell, and taste. Hence, why this phenomenon is often coined a "sixth" sense. Some sciences say that this information is received through the mind, alone. However, it often ridiculed in psychology and wider science—an alleged 'paranormal' or supernatural phenomenon that many believe is best suited to science fiction. Yet, to the surprise of many academics, a significant body of scientific evidence exists which may suggest otherwise!

Etheric Body: This is the body charged by God with the Holy memory of all things lovely and beautiful within the substance of the divine world ... in order that you may bask in that power which one day you will know to its fullest.

Experience: Only by turning inward can you discover bliss and liberation and true peace of the divine. You must experience it yourself, and this will not happen by reading a book, traveling somewhere, or when you listen to any other human being.

Fate: Fate is the real debate. Could it be when you fail to create your own destiny? Try to imagine you were about to run a race ... you know there's a finishing line, but you do not what is going to happen between the start and finish.

Feng Shui: The Ancient Chinese art of placing objects, furnishings, and buildings to create a harmonious and healthy flow of chi (energy/life force that flows around us).

Food: There is a direct correlation with your dietary habits and sleep. The greater amount you consume requires more energy by the body (especially during sleep) to process it ... hence the more tired you can feel. While the body needs food to survive, this has no relation to social or religious background. If you were truly starving and there was a choice of a plate of food and God's presence to appear in front of you, what would you choose to partake/digest? Your self-preservation will kick in! However, the amount you eat on a daily basis is compulsive or conscious in nature. Will you, therefore, embrace this freedom of choice or have you become a slave to this requirement? As the world endures the COVID-19 pandemic it has been scientifically proven that those who are obese have less ability to overcome the virus. The morals and ethics of how we look after our bodies (with food intake and exercise) can be encapsulated in the question ... "How long do we want to live?" To help further, understand that different food can be full of positive, negative, or contain no 'pranic' (life-energy) at all ... which leads to lethargy. Some foods like Honey (with hot water) are so good they break down fat, others dull your nervous system or may stop your bodies sensitivity too. The digestion of everything inside your stomach has various timescales. For example, most fruit takes about three hours, whereas meat could take two to three days! If you could imagine a piece of meat left in the hot sun for the same time it would fester and become full of bacteria. Inside you, the bodies temperature creates the same conditions, so once again the choice to have something like this (rotting flesh) inside you remains. Know too, that *protein* is that what 'protects' you, and food that is not cooked contains the largest amount of protein. Ideally, your diet should therefore contain at least 40% of fruit, vegetables, nuts etcetera. After eating, the most advantageous proportions inside your stomach would be 1/2 food, 1/4 water and 1/4 empty.

Forbearance: An important quality indeed. The spiritual seeker must appreciate that happiness in their life occurs by totally trusting in the universe and remaining in an acceptance mode. This way, one's joy and peace will always remain undisturbed, and you will never feel frustrated, impatient, or let down.

Forgiveness: Is the key to connect with the open door of your own Christ-self. The quality of love is all-encompassing and all-forgiving. Learn to forgive others and most of all yourself, for true healing.

Free will: The discretion to use or not use ... the freedom of 'choice'. The question then arises over how much of your life unfolds automatically or compulsively (if it is not happening the way you want it to) rather than acting with your intelligence ... consciously. In addition, free will was not granted or given power by any governing body or power, other than whim and what you (and God) already are. For such a reason, all your reaction to action, and your cause to the effect can be nothing more than this. Therefore, as you make your way along the journey that we call life ... you—as a soul—can shine as a billion suns, or as a dim light covered by a blanket of hate and doubt.

Gestalt: A structure/concept. According to Gestalt theory, individuals adopt social roles to fulfill their biological needs. It is a humanistic, holistic person-centered form of psychotherapy focused upon a person's present life and challenges—rather than one's past experiences. This is a fluid process in which a pressing need manifests into consciousness in order to be fulfilled. Also stated as a collection of physical, biological, psychological, or symbolic entities that creates a unified concept, configuration or pattern which is greater than the sum of its parts. NB This is an important aspect of Controlled Remote Viewing whereby the 'symbols' collated help to provide a structure of the 'target'.

Glory: Recognise the glory of your own soul, your divine link with the glory of God, creator, universal intelligence. See and feel its glorious reflection within yourself.

Grace: Receiving God's grace can be automatic, but usually follows the effort and endeavour made by the 'seeker'. It requires non-resistance and unconditional acceptance in the reality of our oneness and boundless state.

Guru: 'Gu' means darkness, 'ru' means dispeller. Therefore, a Guru is someone who dispels darkness … to throw light on your very nature of existence.

Happiness: To be happy you must stop finding fault with anything and everything … situations, people, and things. One must surrender to the acceptance of what is because true happiness has no cause behind it. To experience this, you must know yourself by removing all dependence on external situations… which allows you to discover the true 'uncaused' happiness of your real nature—bliss.

Healing: Is a letting-go process… do it every day as you hold and welcome love into your heart. Every day you have the power to express the light of your divinity to any life who needs it. Know that the healing process takes place first in the soul—spiritually and emotionally. Then the mind, mentally and visually … followed by the body, which will always reflect the state of your true and higher self.

Hepatoscopy: Divining from the liver. Opinions differ as to how the state of the liver could act as an omen. It was once considered to be the seat of life, and that where the liver of the animal sacrificed (generally a sheep) was accepted, it took on the character of the deity to whom it was offered. The soul of the animal as seen in the liver … became then a reflector of the soul of the 'god'. On the other hand, the ancient Babylonians viewed the lines and forms of the sheep's liver as reflecting the universe and its history.

Heart: Your heart is a gift from creation. It is the seat of your soul and the very altar of God. Comprehend that inside the heart there is a central chamber, surrounded and protected by a forcefield known as the 'cosmic interval'. This chamber is separated from Matter, and no microscope or probing can ever discover it. Only true vision—when the eyes of the body, soul and mind are in unison can one bear witness to its magnificence. Know that it is the connecting point of the powerful crystal cord of light that descends from your God presence— which sustains the beating of your physical heart. This also gives your life purpose and a reason for integration with the cosmos. Therefore, we must cherish this contact point of 'life' by turning within to pay conscious recognition to it.

Hierarchy of Light: The cosmic Hierarchy is a 'universal chain' of individualized God free beings fulfilling attributes and aspects of God's infinite Selfhood.

Higher Self: A person's spiritual self, their true identity … a focus to many meditation techniques, as opposed to the physical body.

Human being: A definition which defines us. Our consciousness and intellect distinguish us from all other life forms because we know 'how to be'.

Hydromancy: Divination by interpretation of water, observing its colour, ripples and the ebb and flow.

I: Most people—when saying 'I'—are referring to (or thinking of) their body or mind, however 'I' represents our 'Immortal consciousness'.

I AM: You are saying "God in me is" … so that everything you say after these words manifests in our world.

I AM THAT I AM: The name and living presence of 'God' the 'as above so below'. In the West—the path of the Mother—descends. In the East, "OM TAT SAT OM"—the path of the Spirit—ascends. The energy of your being and all that is locked in imperfection becomes a spiral of the ascension and returns to the heart of the God presence.

I Ching: An ancient Chinese type of divination to reveal patterns of change through deep introspection and intuitive thought.

Ichthyomancy: Divination by interpreting the behaviour (or the entrails) of fish.

Identity: Your true identity is part of the cosmos. You have to shift from what the mind believes is just the physical, to that of consciousness.

Without the light, your identity is like a moth drawn to and darting around the flame of truth ... but charring or burning your wings to depart into the abyss of suffering and darkness ... without having attained illumination and liberation.

Immortality: Those of faith and religious persuasion believe the indefinite continuation of a person's existence, even after death. Other opinions state that mental activity is nothing but cerebral activity and as such ... death brings the total end of a person's existence. In truth, immortality is the fruit of sacrifice.

Inspiration: One of the greatest gifts of your divinity is to become the example, the inspiration whereby you move from 'unwillingness' to 'willingness'. God provides you with droplets of truth, those golden nuggets of wisdom, the fragments of creation to stimulate your thoughts and actions to 'create'. Even if you feel that you have not reached the pinnacle, or conversely feel like you have plummeted to the depths ... you retain the ability inside you to inspire

Intention: The idea that is conveyed or intended to be conveyed to the mind by, symbols, language, or action. Intentions keep you in the moment, the aim or purpose for doing what you are doing. When you set an intention, you are determining to act in a certain way. Before setting an intention, it is best to pause and reflect about your what you really need. Perhaps its self-love, being more compassionate towards yourself, or nurturing your inner child? Try to focus an intention to what best meets your needs right now. You can use an intention to be a reminder of how you want to live each day, but in essence they are about how you feel when you do something.

Intuition: Of all the psychic abilities, intuition may well be the most common. sometimes referred to as clairsentience, it is the ability to 'know' things without being told. In fact, intuitive people often make excellent Tarot card readers because this skill gives them an advantage when 'reading' the cards.

Invocation: The act or instance of invoking, a prayer or command to a higher power, deity, spirit, God for assistance, divine guidance, forgiveness, and protection. Sometimes used in the opening of a religious festival. It is also a way of bringing the best out in you.

Journey: The most important journey you can undertake in this lifetime is from being unconscious to conscious. This includes your thoughts, words and deeds and everything within and around you!

Joy: Try to bring a feeling of lightness to your heart and a renewed joy in living. Laughter and joyous love will bring out the child in you, transmuting any feelings of negativity and heaviness within you. Make your days joyful and watch the world around change for the better! In reality, your true accomplishment is the joy you cause in the 'heart' of God ... and 'joy' derived from service reacts upon the 'body' and helps to keep you free from disease too.

Karma: Literally means 'Action' and is of your own making. Most of your actions are unconscious, played out through one's physical, mental, emotional and life-energy. Also believed to be the totality of a person's actions and conduct and memory during successive incarnations or regarded as cause and effect that may influence their destiny. Karma is also considered to be a law or principle through which such influence is believed to operate ... fate resulting from one's previous actions. However, counteracting a 'fate/destiny' scenario, it is incredibly empowering to know that each day is our own making. Misery or joy are the choice which affects the very nature of our lives. Therefore, you are responsible for your own future ... it is in your own hands!

Labyrinth: Most think of a labyrinth as a maze, but a maze is a puzzle to be solved with twists and turns, designed to lose your way. A labyrinth has no blind alleys ... and with only one way in and out it helps you find your way! It is an ancient spiritual tool dating back 4000 years or more, designed for contemplation, increased wisdom, discernment and for spiritual transformation. They are usually formed as a circle with a singular path which is formed by a range of materials ... creating a sacred space. Often found in the architecture of old churches, coastlines, forests etc. Regarding the symbol itself, the classical design has an association with Christianity. A cross is the starting point surrounded by seven loops ... which can also resemble those U-turns we all seem to experience in our lives. It is easy for the mind to imagine these in terms of being positive or negative, but it can represent a time of immense growth and personal change ... both physically and spiritually. One popular aspect to walking a labyrinth is to break the process down in to 4 key elements.

- Positive—Remembering: Before you walk, gather your thoughts, and remember you are blessed. You and all of creation are a blessing from God/the divine/the source.

- Negative—Releasing: You must let go. Quieten the mind, release your frustrations, concerns, fears both at the entrance and at the center of the labyrinth.

- Creativity—Receiving: Now you have released or emptied (I like brain dumped) you have the space to receive the guidance you need from creation/spirit/God. This might be a sense of wholeness, feeling loved, inner quietness and peace or even an enlightened experience.

- Transformation—Resolving: This begins when you leave the center. You return on the same path out of the labyrinth and should now feel able to resolve an issue, knowing the way forward. This can be the springboard to the new 'you', almost like a reawakening or being reborn ... to live the truth of 'you'.

Light: The highest frequency we know. Your physical eyes can only see that which is stopped by light. However, the pure element of the 'I' bears witness to all creation because it sees without being tarnished by memory, and views everything exactly the way it is. Jesus once said, "The light of the body is eye (I). If therefore thine eye (I) be single, thy whole body shall be full of light."

Lithomancy: Divination using crystals or semi-precious stones, either by interpreting the light from them … or by casting them and interpreting their placement as they fall.

Logic: Try not to get bogged down or become a slave to logic and the reasoning/propositions and conclusions of others. Validate the truth of your reality through your own experiences, for the cosmos is here and now!

Love: Love is the way you are. Love enables us to fulfil the destiny of the soul in conscious outer manifestation—a just and merciful compassion that is always rewarded by individual creative fulfilment. Through the power of love, man learns how they may impart into others the beauty and compassion that they have received from God. Love does not need to have sustenance from anyone, therefore, if you are loving … it spreads!

Manifesting: Bringing your desires and aspirations into being … through focusing your thoughts and energy. The manifestation process is the transmutation of thought into the physical world. It can help you bring into real life the things you want, whether that is love, improved health, money etc. It is important to note that is not so much about getting, but ore about becoming. In essence, when you let go of the lack, you become abundant. Likewise, when you give … so shall you receive. Note that manifestation's origins stem from spirituality and religion, because if something spiritual transcends into reality, it is said to be a manifestation. Remember, you need to believe and keep receptive!

Mantra: A word or formula (often in Sanskrit). They attune you and govern the release or attraction of life-energy, which becomes deposited in your aura. This expands over time, gaining momentum. For example, this powerful mantra from India "OM NANORA RIJA NIYA" tunes oneself with the infinite. "O infinite God, I want your will to be done in me".

Meditation: Practiced for millennia, and originally intended to develop spiritual understanding, awareness, and direct experience of ultimate reality. Although an important spiritual practice in many religions and traditions, it can be practiced regardless of someone's religious or cultural background. It can be used with other forms of medical treatment, and as a complementary therapy for the many stress-related conditions. Types of meditation include concentration, movement, mindfulness, and transcendental. When you meditate you are just withdrawing support from your personality, you are creating a distance between your true self and your mind … in essence, observing from an elevated, clearer viewpoint. In fact, the state of meditation is wherever and whenever you place yourself in touch with God!

Metaphysical senses: The four metaphysical senses are deemed as the following … Clairsentience (clear feeling), Clairvoyance (clear seeing), Clairaudience (clear hearing), and Claircognizance (clear knowing).

Metoposcopy: Divination through interpreting the lines and wrinkles in the forehead. (Don't try it on someone whose had botox though).

Mind: Eastern philosophy and wisdom state there are 16 segments to the mind. The 4 main 'parts' relate to intellect, identity, memory (evolutionary and genetic) and pure intelligence. It encapsulates our thoughts and emotions. NB. People often refer to their 'monkey' mind during meditation, but our purpose is to liberate it, not control it!

Mind Fasting: Bracketing any distracting or disturbing thoughts aside so we can 'fast' from thinking about them while we listen to God. (See also Silence and stillness).

Mindfulness: Reconnecting with our bodies, and the sensations they experience. Becoming aware of our thoughts and feelings through our senses—knowing what is going on inside and around ourselves—at any given moment.

Numerology: A form of divination that assigns numeric values to birthdates and names and then uses those values to define an individual's personal characteristics, aptitudes, and life path.

English letter numeric values:

A-I	J-R	S-Z
A = 1	J = 10 (1)	S = 19 (10) (1)
B = 2	K = 11 (2)	T = 20 (2)
C = 3	L = 12 (3)	U = 21 (3)
D = 4	M = 13 (4)	V = 22 (4)
E = 5	N = 14 (5)	W = 23 (5)
F = 6	O = 15 (6)	X = 24 (6)
G = 7	P = 16 (7)	Y = 25 (7)
H = 8	Q = 17 (8)	Z = 26 (8)
I = 9	R = 18 (9)	

And here's a spooky coincidence...

World war I   Date 28/7/1914   28+7+19+14 = **68**

World War II   Date   1/9/1939   1+9+19+39 = **68**

Invasion of Ukraine Date 24/2/2022   24+2+20+22 = **68**

Necromancy: Consulting the dead.

Omnipotent: Having unlimited or Universal power, authority, or force; all-powerful.

Omnipresent: The state of being everywhere at once. All-pervading, Universal, ever-present.

Omniscient: Having total knowledge, knowing everything. All-knowing, all-seeing, wise.

Oneiromancy: Divination through the interpretation of dreams. (See dreams)

Oracle: Contacting spirits or gods.

Ouija: Divination with the use of a Ouija Board, a board printed with the alphabet and numbers and using a planchette to spell out messages. I'd be very careful using this. Prayers of protection prior to its use are the order of the day … because you just don't know what sort of negativity/dark energies you will experience/bring forth.

Palmistry/Palm reading: Divination through reading and interpreting the lines and structure of the hand.

Pallomancy: Divination using a pendulum. Easy to make you own with a bit of string and a key/small stone/jewel. You can ask for yes/no answers to your questions with a clockwise/anticlockwise rotation.

Path: It does not matter what route you take if you are just constantly striving for 'more'. Know that you will never reach the destination if you continually require and crave more love, more money, more success etcetera. Only the pathless path brings you the perception, the clarity and the focus needed to liberate and experience perpetual bliss.

Patience: Recognise and feel the principle of patience to release tension in the mind and body and your life. With greater awareness, an increase in your level of endurance and ability to suffer restlessness and annoyance without complaint.

Pegomancy: The interpretation of sacred waters such as wells, springs, pools, or a fountain.

Personality: This is the one and the only real difference between each human being. It reflects and manifests as our likes and dislikes in every way and form imaginable … and thus induces bondage.

Physiognomy: Divining a person's character through interpreting the features of his/her face.

Precognition: Future events observed in a past dream. Also called pre-science, future vision of future insight … and is a claimed psychic ability to see future events. Sometimes you have a 'key', perhaps a symbol or a feeling by which to identify them … like myself, with the 'lightening flashes', or a newspaper image described in this book.

There are few different classifications. First, let's look at what's often referred to as **Lower Order precognitive dreams**:

1) Symbolic Precognitive dreams: This is one of the most difficult to identify. Here dream symbolism selects the precognitive information which is not realised until the actual event. These can either match or exaggerate the future event when it actualizes. Imagine a complex dream and in it you meet a large man with black hair wearing a yellow coat. This might be the only symbolism to be retained from the dream, everything else has become blurred by one's perception and/or reduced awareness in the dream itself.

2) Third-person precognitive dreams: This type can take on literal and symbolic similarities. However, you are not part of the dream itself but are observing the dream setting or location from a third person point of view.

3) Probabilistic precognitive dreams: Of course, probability will play a role when the dream content precedes the future information/data. Something takes place in 'real' time whereby someone has made a certain choice **after** the dream has taken place, which then causes the event to change in some way. So, in the example above, the large man with black hair is later seen in real life … but he is wearing a green coat. The issue here is one might think it just a coincidence rather than precognitive. These three issues highlight how memory and awareness, and perception and probability can all impact the resulting future event, compared to what is written in your dream log/journal or 'remembered'. Now then, moving on to **Higher Order precognitive dreams**.

1) A Literal Precognitive dream is in literal detail. Here it becomes more difficult to pass off such dreams as a coincidence if the person has a high degree of clarity and detail. Hence, the relationship between the future event and the dreamer is very strong and their memory of the dream matches the event in eerie detail. These dreams function from first-person

perspective whereby he or she is experiencing the future event itself. Feelings and thoughts and what are sensed are all likely to match an event that becomes realized.

2) Lucid Precognitive Dreams. These are uncommon though are deemed to be either Active or Ambient. (Terms coined by Robert Waggoner of the ISAD-International Association for the Study of Dreams). If future data is being observed then it can be possible to become lucid (where one is aware of dreaming) during a precognitive dream, but this doesn't mean the person knows this at the time. They just go with the flow … hence 'ambient'. (The dreamer won't realize this fact until the event occurs). Active Lucid precognitive dreams are quite bizarre because they allow the dreamer to control elements of dream content. It is possible to induce something into the dream when the dreamer realizes they're dreaming.

While such categories aren't definitive, I hope they will give you a better idea into this weird phenomenon. Perhaps you can relate your own precognitive experiences with them too.

Premonitions: The result from what can only be called extra-sensory perception … be it a vision, a gut feeling, or another experience that grants you knowledge of things that haven't happened yet. These experiences can be hard to recognize, as you won't realize you've had one of these dreams (or visions) until the event actually occurs. That said, premonition dreams are more common than you might think.

Prophecy: Prediction, forecast, insight … the unconscious deduction from subliminal perception on a causal chain. A message claimed by a person (typically a prophet) to have been communicated to them by a deity. Such messages usually involve inspiration, interpretation of dreams, or revelation of divine will concerning the prophet's contemporary world and/or an extraordinary knowledge of events to come in the future.

Purification: A high dimensional frequency which can operate at a causal body level throughout the subtle bodies (mind, etheric, physical, and emotional), and the auric field. This transmutes lower energies and allows a new feeling of purity to filter through the conscious mind.

Pyromancy: The art of divination using fire, which is deeply rooted in ancient Greek mythology. Fire has always been considered an important part of our lives and therefore been given a high position in the so-called 'occult' world. So, you simply gaze into the fire or even just a candle flame. It is believed this provides an easier and clearer picture of what we wish to see more than any other technique. It was thought to be a good omen if the fire started easily, but if it was hard to kindle, it was not a good sign at all. There are several other divination methods which fall under pyromancy and all use fire in some way. This might involve burning a specific substance. These include capnomancy (which is divination by smoke), alomancy (divination in which salt is thrown into fire), daphnomancy (the burning of laurel leaves), botanomancy (burning of various leaves) and sideromancy (burning straws) and causimomancy (observing objects placed in a fire).

Psychic: The term being psychic refers to one's 'abilities' (gaining knowledge without 'assumptions or conscious reasoning') ... utilising universal energy through intuition, an inner sense of knowing and unconscious cognition to gain information.

Psychometry: Divination through touching or handling an object.

Psychomancy: Divination through the interpretation of a person's soul, i.e., their values and beliefs ... hence a soul 'reading'.

Remote Viewing: The psychic phenomenon of projecting your mind to receive information without leaving the body. Similar to clairvoyance, remote viewing is the ability to sense accurate details and information regarding location, event or even a person without utilizing any obvious means or any of the physical senses. This is a skill you can learn regardless of your natural psychic receptivity! (Not to be confused with astral projection where the practitioner leaves their body).

In World War II, the Soviets believed the U.S. Military were using psychic communications and started their own training programmes. The U.S Government learned of these and later in the 1970s (during the cold war), the CIA had training programmes of their own at the SRI (Stanford Research Institute). Originally, they wanted to prove it wasn't possible and couldn't exist. Physicists Hal Putoff and Russell Targ worked there determining whether ESP was real or not. They invited Ingo Swann of New York City (a psychic and scientist who demonstrated an ability in this phenomenon) and after they conducted several tests, the Remote Viewing programme was born. It was Ingo who devised 'Controlled' RV using map co-ordinates and a 6 stage system … a set of structural protocols designed to help you discover the process and control your intuition. Rather than using nouns to describe what you perceive; you start by describing your perceptions … without trying to identify anything about what they mean. You use basic gestalts to give you the overall concept/ components of the target site. Whether its manmade, land, water, living (elements of 'life'), space/air, energy/motion or natural. Once accustomed and proficient in these, you proceed to smells, temperature, and also shapes and sizes too. You are opening the aperture of your perception through your subconsciousness and thereby resist the temptation to draw what you think are conclusions based on logical analysis. Bizarrely, the fainter or fuzzier your perception the greater the likelihood of accuracy!

Whether or not psychic espionage is still be going on in the world I'm not sure, but this method of utilising one's intuition and psychic abilities has helped people to solve crime, find objects, chose a place to live, decide what job to go for and many other applications … so I guess anything is possible! So, why not investigate CRV further and try it for yourself? In any case, I urge you to open the lines of communication between your subconscious and conscious mind and develop this relationship.

Responsibility: One could say this is our ability to respond to everything that occurs within and outside of us. In real terms, our ability to respond to any given situation is limitless, whereas our ability to act is limited. It is the simplest way to express our divinity too.

Rhabdomancy: Divination with the use of a divining rod.

Runes: The original meaning of the word rune is 'secret, or something hidden'. It is widely believed that the early runes were used in magic, as magical signs for divination, however, we have no direct evidence of this. They were also considered to be a gift from the 'gods' specifically from the king of the gods, Odin ... the 'all father', and for this reason, they were venerated and cast with extreme caution and respect for their metaphysical qualities and divine origin.

You can make your own set of Runes very easily. I collected small pebbles and the like from various beaches ... choosing those that resonated within me ... perhaps for their individual shape or colour which had caught my eye. I even painted the symbols on them with my wife's nail polish! I still have them from the late 1990's, although haven't 'read' them for many years.

So, rune meanings are applied by using these symbols; each stone has a symbol which is based on an ancient alphabet. Each one holds specific meaning and when you ask a question and pull out a rune from the bag (in response to your question), you will receive the appropriate advice in symbol form. Traditionally, to cast runes, you spread out a white cloth. Then with eyes closed, pick three runes from the bag, place them on the cloth and predict the outcome of a venture or answer a question, based on their interpretations. Alternatively, try what's called the 'PRIMSTAVE' reading ... which is picking five runes and analyzing them as follows: 1) Overview of the situation. 2) The challenge 3) Course of action called for. 4) The sacrifice. 5) Evolved situation. Today, this 'occult' knowledge has come a long way, and many people around the world seek help of these ancient symbols, to find solutions for their problems.

The runic alphabet typically consists of 24 runes, each inscribed with its own magical symbol, and one blank rune called 'Odin's rune'. The blank rune represents that which cannot or must not be known about the future. When it comes up in rune reading or spread, it is the equivalent of drawing a blank. The most popular and oldest set of runic alphabets is the *Elder Futhark*, Here's a breakdown of the meanings: **Fehu:** Cattle/Wealth,

Uruz: Ox/power and strength, **Thurisaz:** Giant/force, **Ansuz:** Message, **Raidho:** Journey, **Kaunaz:** Fire/Torch, **Gebo:** Gift/spirit of giving, **Wunjo:** Joy/happiness, **Hagalaz:** Hail/change/storm or calm, **Nauthiz:** Needs, **Isa:** Ice/freezing or suspension of plans, **Jera:** Harvest/fruit of labour, **Eihwaz:** Yew/fortitude against external forces, **Perthro:** Destiny/mystery and chance, **Algiz:** Elk/protection ... aware of surroundings, **Sowelo:** Sun/ the rising or awakening of one's spirit from darkness. **Tiwaz:** Honor, justice, bravery, **Berkano:** Birth and rebirth, **Ehwaz:** Horse/travel, **Mannaz:** Mankind/Spirit of humanity, **Laguz:** Water/ ebb and flow, **Ingwaz:** Earth/ New beginnings, **Dagaz:** New dawn/hope, **Othala:** Ancestral property, inheritance. Know that if a rune is upside down, then it indicates the reverse/opposite of its meaning.

Sceptics/Skeptics: Those experiencing doubt or question ... who believe psychic experiences have a simple if logical explanation. Remember, even if you disbelieve in such philosophical concepts/phenomena, it does not mean you cannot experience or develop them!

Scrying: The word "scrying" means to reveal or to perceive. Our ancestors used the clouds during the day and the reflection of the moon in a puddle of water at night to scry. To be a scryer, you are crossing over to another consciousness, a mystical plain, and leaving behind your conscious mind. The formal definition being: 'Scrying is the art of gazing into a transparent, translucent, or otherwise reflective object'. Examples include Crystal ball gazing, Crystal gazing, Fires Scrying, Ink Scrying, Mirror Scrying, Smoke Scrying, Water Scrying and even Wine Scrying ... whereby we go beyond the physical eyes and letting the inner psychic eye open allowing you to receive visions and information. Scrying is a learned skill. The scryer attempts to interpret the images that come up in the reflective surface, which, if they want to hone this skill and read with accuracy, should involve a lot of practice. One important thing to remember here (prior to attempting such things) is to ask your spirit guides (and/or pray) for protection. You would never know what energies you are invoking during the process. That said, it may well present you with the opportunities to impart messages, lessons, warnings, and divine wisdom.

Selenomancy: Divination of the appearance and various phases of the moon.

Self-realization: The expression used in psychology, spirituality, and Eastern religions. Can be defined as the fulfilment by oneself of the possibilities of one's character, personality, potential, and Divinity. To become 'realised' means you finally perceive what is already there! Please note ... that the instruments of your perception are all outward bound, but the seat of experience is within you.

Senses: Nature has allowed you to live life through the sense organs. Eyes provide sight to beautiful scenes and all your surroundings. Ears enable sound and melody to soothe or stir your emotions. The nose permits the aroma and fragrances of creation to ignite your imagination. Taste enables you to savour nutritious food which give life and health to the body. Touch gives you the opportunity to know and feel personal contact. However, the common theme with each sense is that they all crave and desire ... which only leads to your likes and dislikes creating bondage. You must, therefore, use your intelligence to control the mind and take charge of the senses for spiritual life ...and make them your servants and not your masters! A true seeker will only become fulfilled this way to experience eternal bliss. N.B. An old Indian metaphor captures this perfectly, "Use the intellect-charioteer to take charge of the reins of the mind and your sense-horses ... if you want to reach the destination of Self-realisation".

Silence: Is that which is NOT the basis of sound. Keeping silent has an immensely powerful impact on your life ... a representation of 'nothingness'. Many guides also state you should reduce what you say by 50% ... and even my wife says I talk too much! Remember, silence is the speech of the spiritual seeker.

Signs: One may deem 'signs' as a spiritual language. What I am referring to is the imagery, symbols, sounds or any information that comes from our spirit guides who watch over us all ... forms of communication as it were. Spirit will use any means at their disposal to convey what you are meant to hear, see, or feel. Some call this assistance from the 'other' side ... heaven if you like. One of my own favourite examples of this occurred when I was leaving a job in financial services—which in the end I started to loathe. It was a very stressful time after going through much personal upheaval and loss. I was about to drive away from the office for the last time. The sun was shining in a clear blue sky. I opened the car window and took a deep sigh of breath. Turning on the car radio, a chorus of a song by Ultra Nate bellowed out ... 'Cause you're free, to do what you want to do. You've got to live your life, do want you want to do.' There are many 'signs' you may know of, like a white feather falling at your feet or even smelling the perfume or aftershave of a loved one who has crossed over. These are but gentle, wonderful reminders that we are all watched over and loved. Remember everything is energy/God. And love is the most powerful force in creation. If you are ever in doubt over your divine connection with a loved one ... think of an object, an image, a place or even a feeling that connects you both. Something simple would suffice. Ask the universe for a sign and it will come. Allow the universe to work through you with an open mind and heart, and it will speak back—just be ready to receive it!

Sleep: It is well known that the body rejuvenates and even repairs itself during sleep, but whether the average human being requires 8 hours is debatable. Of course, there may be hormonal issues in play which affect the need for even more sleep too, but it is important to cut down on it. Try to arise after 5 or 6 hours, or at least as soon as you awake. This might seem difficult to action, but this may allow you to experience another 10 or more years of life! So, if by the alarm clock or by naturally waking with the dawn chorus, do not just turn over ... thinking 'I love my bed', or that you cannot get up citing 'you need to recharge the batteries'. Know it is not so much physical rest you require but more the time to ease the restless mind to re-awaken the divinity within you. Therefore, will you stand by your bed and gaze upon the imprint of your slumber? Will you continue to resist life's tasks and tests, or grasp the opportunities presenting themselves in a new day? Why not embrace your 'aliveness' to bring joy into your life and all those around you too? In reality, sleep is a death state which you enter into through instalments (inertia), whereas life is dynamic. Remember, you cannot 'enjoy' sleep, but to rest—and the time for restfulness—is the basis of all your activity.

Sojourn: A temporary stay; a brief period of residence.

Soul: The soul is not the object of intellect …but the very source of your intellect!

Spirit world: Is real, but not always innocent. This is why whenever you are in contact with the 'other side', it is important to question who and what they are. Clarify their purpose. They will not mind if they are genuine and loving. According to Scripture, those spirits that are not the Holy Spirit or angels are evil spirit. On rare occasions, I have been privileged (during dream state) to assist in spirit rescue work. This involves venturing into deep darkness and helping to raise another 'soul' towards their reality … 'light'.

Spiritual Healing: Spiritual healing has been a principle of Spiritualism since its establishment as a religion. However, it differs from faith healing in that the patient need have no faith in the treatment. Faith healers also claim instant cures, while in Spiritual healing the cures are rarely instantaneous. In addition, rather than belief in divine intervention, the Spiritual healer believes that spirits work through him or her to energize and heal the patient. Over the years I have been blessed to work for 'spirit' this way. This privilege is a gift that I believe we all possess, and I always found that when healing flowed through me, the recipient could either feel warmth or even coolness … depending on the condition that was being treated. Some describe the energy that comes through as like a sticky candyfloss feeling. I would always ground myself as it would feel like negativity … blackness which would then flow back through my arms. On a friend who was about to leave their mortal coil, I nearly puked up … it was so 'bad' that I almost passed out. Basically, healing is love …

from spirit, through spirit and to spirit for our emotional, mental, and physical 'bodies' we possess.

Spiritual seeker: Many people understand that being a seeker involves making a total and absolute surrender to 'life' by accepting whatever comes their way. However, when transformation, guidance, and the materialisation of what is sought does not occur ... grave doubt may arise. Then, further obstacles or suffering will usually generate the question, "Why me?" or "Why is it happening?" But this only creates a further barrier, so it is crucial not to think or ask the 'why' question! If you can only transcend the need for any clarification in all your experiences (whether deemed 'good', 'bad', or indifferent) this will finally allow the Universal consciousness and life-energy to resolve the situation for your higher good and at the earliest opportunity too.

Spiritualism: The three main aspects are ... the survival of the spirit after death, the ongoing concern of the deceased (spirits) for the living, and also the ability of those spirits to communicate with the living through a medium (a person who serves as an intermediary between the spirits and the living).

Spirituality: Going beyond the boundary of the body/senses. You experience the reality past the physical presence, and in life, react with your intelligence consciously. In essence, spiritual life is transformation!

Stillness: Being still empowers you because it allows you to be in touch with another dimension. When you are consciously 'still', the energy you access becomes a link between the non-physical and physical elements of your existence ... so you are able to witness the reality of life in its entirety. In essence, you leave your perception of a limited identity behind to see and experience the truth. Understand that stillness is not sleep, which is unconscious slumber.

Synchronicity: Carl Jung (the Swiss psychoanalyst) coined this phrase as a 'meaningful coincidence'. It demonstrates our innate and active and divine connection with each other and everything around us. You think of someone, and they just happen to ring you. You might be humming a tune or singing your favourite song and then it starts playing on the radio. Heck, even the other day I saw part of a BBC television quiz show. A contestant was asked to name one of the squares between two positions on a traditional monopoly board. I shouted to my wife, "Vine Street", and within a second the contestant said, 'Vine Steet' as well! Are these occurrences plain random or purposeful in design? What do you believe?

Taromancy: Divination by using a deck of Tarot Cards

Tarot: Tarot cards are small, paper cards that come in a deck, similar to playing cards, and are used for divinatory purposes. Thought to at least date from the mid-15th century in various parts of Europe ... to play games such as Italian tarocchini, French tarot and Austrian Königrufen, many of which are still played today. Each Tarot deck has the same number of cards (78). Within each deck there are four suits—called the minor arcana—and another set of 22 cards—called the major arcana. Each card represents a different archetypal being or lesson. A person shuffles the cards, then lays them out in a Tarot card 'spread'. One should look beyond the obvious answers and pay attention to the reversed Tarot cards as their meaning can turn your answers in a different direction.

Tasseography/Tasseomancy: This is the divination through the reading of tea leaves, coffee grounds, or even wine sediments.

Theriomancy: Divination through the interpretation of the movements of groups of animals.

Time: Is the only proof of the existence of 'matter', however, seconds, minutes and hours are not your true pillars of creation. It is not how little or how much time you have, but what you do with it that counts. When you are joyful, time will seem to disappear, when you are miserable ... a day can feel like eternity. When you turn inward and have no sense of body, you detach yourself from the clock face and the unreal develops into reality. When you truly accept the awareness and the inevitability of the 'moment', all suffering is gone. Understand everything in creation is in this moment, whereas your mind thinks of the future (imagination) and the past (memory). So, one must be conscious and live in the moment, for it is only this moment which is inevitable!

Transformation: Nothing of the old 'you' should remain—in contrast to improvement, which is just a 'change.' As such, the object of your desires may alter your destination, but only when you stop seeking/asking/ striving for what you do not have can you change the inner process of one's life. By transformation, you shift oneself to a completely new dimension of perception and experience ... hence 'self-transformation'.

Tranquillity: When the subtle vibrations which surround the body become disturbed, you feel stressed. You need to combat this, so take the mind elsewhere. Visualise somewhere calm, perhaps by a still lake or a special place held dear to your heart. Allow peace to wash over you and bring tranquillity to your body, thoughts, and consciousness.

Truth: Can only be perceived and experienced, it cannot be interpreted.

Turning inward: When you sit still in silence, there is an opportunity to 'experience' your reality beyond the senses. In doing so, what you have previously classed as your identity (which were bound by one's sex, race, religion, and beliefs), will break free and lose its limitations.

Unconditional love: This form of love is not emotional and has no strings or ties. It is the only true healing power, so try to allow your heart to be activated in this way.

Unity: Is divinity.

Urticariaomancy: Divination by the location of an itch. Ever had itchy palms ... you'll get money or if your nose itches, someone is thinking about you!

Vibration and energy: The resonance of your true 'self'. We are all at different stages of spiritual development, so the intensity of reverberation (sound) within would indicate the energy level you have reached. Every substance has its own frequency, its own keynote. Every sound has form, and every form has sound.

Visualisation: A mental image, like one's visual perception.

Wheel of Fortune: The Wheel of Fortune turns forevermore, seemingly to communicate that life is made up of so-called good and bad times, and that the cycle is one we cannot control. Therefore, in essence … it appears that no one on earth can avoid what is fated. In Tarot, it is generally an indicator of luck or destiny and has a deeply rooted connection to Greek mythology and the three women known as the 'Fates'. If the card is upright, it can indicate chance, destiny and fate, karma, turning points and life cycles. If reversed, upheaval, unwelcome change, lousy 'luck', setbacks, and the influence of external forces. Or … simply a yes or no answer! NB. A common aspect to most interpretations of this card is to introduce an element of change in the querent's life.

Wisdom: 'Wise dominion' … wisdom to nourish the mind—for illumination and the right use of the knowledge of Universal law.

Words: On this journey called 'life' it is important to live in truth, so try speaking what you feel and act what you speak.

Yoga: A group of physical, mental, and spiritual practices or disciplines which originated in ancient India. One of six Astika schools of Hindu philosophical traditions. In the West, it is often seen as just bending of the body, for a better posture or exercise … but in the East, it is a contemporary science, vitally relevant to our times.

Further Reading

You will find your own guidance and inspiration every day, week, month, or year as nothing in life is ever by 'chance'. Each Lesson will simply be the most appropriate for your needs at that time, helping you to find inner peace and balance, as well as your own spiritual education, growth and understanding. Here is a selection of my favourite books and authors, which I hope you will enjoy reading too.

Sai Baba Gita-
The Way to Self-Realization and Liberation in this age.
By Al Drucker
ISBN 0-9638449-0-3

Conversations with God
By Neale Donald Walsh
Book 1 - ISBN 0-340-69325-8
Book 2 - ISBN 0-340-76544-5
Book 3 - ISBN 0-340-76545-3

The Message of a Master
By John McDonald
ISBN 0-931432-95-2

The Celestine Prophecy- An Adventure
By James Redfield
ISBN 0-533-40902-6

Anastasia- The Ringing Cedar series -Book 1
By Vladimir Megre
ISBN 978-0-9801812-0-3

A Course in Miracles
By The Foundation for Inner Peace
ISBN 0-670-86975-9

The Winds of Change
By Stephanie J. King
ISBN 978-0954242169

The Day my life changed
By Carmel Reilly
ISBN 978-1-84509-420-1

Confessions of a Pilgrim
Bu Paulo Coelho
ISBN 0-7225-3293-8

A Mind of your Own
By Betty Shine
ISBN 0-00-255894-7

Angel Inspiration
By Diana Cooper
ISBN 0-340-73323-3

Chicken Soup for the Soul
By Jack Canfield and Mark Victor Hansen
ISBN 0-09185-428-8

The Complete Book of Dreams
By Edwin Raphael
ISBN 0-572-01714-6

The Bible Code
By Michael Drosnin
ISBN 0-297-82994-7

The Secret
By Rhonda Byrne
ISBN: 978-1847370297

Noah Finn & the Art of Suicide
By E. Rachael Hardcastle
ISBN: 978-1999968816

Noah Finn & the Art of Conception
By E. Rachael Hardcastle
ISBN: 978-1999968861

Evolving on Purpose
By Soul Valley Publishing
ISBN: 978-1739993603

Acknowledgements

To my wife Caroline for all her love, support, and encouragement ... and for all those of love and light and truth who connect through my speaking heart.

About the Author

David has helped to conduct spiritual development and healing circles for over 25 years. He has also been a guest speaker—sharing his enlightened experiences to promote 'oneness'—at various Mind, Body, and Spirit engagements in the UK.

Through inner-dictation, dream interpretation, meditation, mindfulness, precognition, and healing, the books he co-writes with 'Spirit' provide you with the foundation to discover your own path of truth. With a renewed sense of purpose, the spiritual guidance and education you receive can help you reach the goal of self-realization and bliss within the permanence of love and light.

David is tee-total and a vegetarian who loves the sunshine, nature, animals, and his wife!

Also by David Knight

Pathway

Deliverance of Love, Light and Truth

I Am I: The Indweller of Your Heart—Book One

I Am I: The Indweller of Your Heart—Book Two

I Am I: The Indweller of Your Heart—Book Three

I Am I: The Indweller of Your Heart— Collection

Leave the Body Behind—Sojourns of the Soul

A Pocket Full of God

Rhyme & Reason

An Invitation/Free book

If you enjoyed reading, FORESIGHT you can download
Deliverance of Love, Light, and Truth for free,
when you join David's mission for a 'full and blissful life'.

To learn more, visit:
http://www.AscensionForYou.com

Follow us on:

Facebook: facebook.com/ascensionforyou

or

Twitter: https://twitter.com/ascensionforyou

… and become part of our community who love to receive uplifting messages for the heart and soul!

Want to let others know what you think?
Please make your opinion known by leaving a 'star rating' with one-click on Amazon.com or Amazon.co.uk and/or a review at your favorite online retailer. Thank you!